Visualization

Use Your Imagination Skills To Visualize And Manifest Your Goals And Dreams

(Achieve Your Goals Through Meditation And Positive Thinking)

Peter Cleary

Published By **Regina Loviusher**

Peter Cleary

All Rights Reserved

Visualization: Use Your Imagination Skills to Visualize and Manifest Your Goals and Dreams (Achieve Your Goals Through Meditation and Positive Thinking)

ISBN 978-1-77485-979-7

No part of this guidebook shall be reproduced in any form without permission in writing from the publisher except in the case of brief quotations embodied in critical articles or reviews.

Legal & Disclaimer

The information contained in this ebook is not designed to replace or take the place of any form of medicine or professional medical advice. The information in this ebook has been provided for educational & entertainment purposes only.

The information contained in this book has been compiled from sources deemed reliable, and it is accurate to the best of the Author's knowledge; however, the Author cannot guarantee its accuracy and validity and cannot be held liable for any errors or omissions. Changes are periodically made to this book. You must consult your doctor or get professional medical advice before using any of the suggested remedies, techniques, or information in this book.

Upon using the information contained in this book, you agree to hold harmless the Author from and against any damages, costs, and expenses, including any legal fees potentially resulting from the application of any of the information provided by this guide. This disclaimer applies to any damages or injury caused by the use and application, whether directly or indirectly, of any advice or information presented, whether for breach of contract, tort, negligence, personal injury, criminal intent, or under any other cause of action.

You agree to accept all risks of using the information presented inside this book. You need to consult a professional medical practitioner in order to ensure you are both able and healthy enough to participate in this program.

Table Of Contents

Chapter 1: Creative Visualization – What It Is...... 1

Chapter 2: The Benefits Of Creative Visualization 9

Chapter 3: How Visualization Can Help You Make Your Plans A Reality 21

Chapter 4: Meditation Skills To Help With Visualization 28

Chapter 5: Why Do You Need To Incorporate Visualization Into Your Life? What Is The Easiest Way? 34

Chapter 6: Visualization Techniques 41

Chapter 7: The Commitment.............................. 54

Chapter 8: Uncovering Your Creativity With Auto-Suggestion 59

Chapter 9: Lucid Dreaming; The Practicalities ... 66

Chapter 10: Visualization Techniques & Exercises You Should Be Knowledgeable........................... 72

Chapter 11: My Secret To Happiness 76

Chapter 12: Unleashing The Amazing Power Of Meditation And How It Can Literally Help Your Brain Explode With Creativity 81

Chapter 13: Relaxed Mind By Reaching Alpha Brainwaves 85

Chapter 14: Butterfly Visualization 91

Chapter 15: How To Make Visualization Work For You 95

Chapter 16: Shape Shift And Transform Your Lives 102

Chapter 17: Procrastination & Stagnation: Why Our Lives Are Stagnated 117

Chapter 18: Mind & Health 123

Chapter 19: The Elements Of The Unique Sub-Conscious Mind 133

Chapter 20: Illustration Of Creative Visualization By Wallace Wattles 140

Chapter 21: Mobile Web And The Internet: The Advancement Of The Internet 143

Chapter 22: Why Should You Get Used To Changes 149

Chapter 23: Different Types Creative Thinking 163

Chapter 24: Increase Productivity By Creating Specific Habits 169

Chapter 25: The Pickles Must Be Held 173

Chapter 1: Creative Visualization – What It Is

Creative visualization uses your imagination to imagine and create scenarios in your head. To use visualization techniques, you create a mental image of something. Then you focus on the scenario or image for a time. Creative visualization is based on a belief that by altering your thoughts or perceptions you can influence the outside world. Many influential, successful and wealthy people believe that by visualizing certain scenarios and behaviours, you can alter the energy patterns to help you reach your goals faster.

Converting dreams into reality

You can make any dream or goal come true with creative visualization. Consider your greatest accomplishment. You remember how fulfilling it felt to be in the midst of all your achievements? Recall the time you felt the desire to achieve your goal was just an idea or seed in your head. What thoughts were you having back then? What were your thoughts? Were you worried and scared, or optimistic and exuberant? Do you imagine success or failure? Are you imagining yourself on the podium, in last place, or on top?

When you first started to think about this goal, it was as if it had been achieved. This is called creative visualization. You can tell your subconscious mind what you want by repeatedly visualizing a person, object or situation. Creative visualization does not require magic. Instead, it's a natural process.

How It Works and Why

Your subconscious mind will recognize the thoughts you repeat most often and change your mind. This is followed by changes in your actions, habits, and mind. This puts you in touch with new situations, situations, or people. Your thoughts have a creative power that can change your life. It is believed that thoughts are able to move between minds and that if they are strong enough others can take them unconsciously.

It is important for people to know that thoughts can be energy. Thoughts have the power to alter the environment and the energy balance. People repeat specific thoughts often. They focus their thoughts on their environment and present situation, and so create and recreate similar circumstances and events. This process does not change the current status quo or "world". You can make the film different by changing your thoughts. If you imagine different situations or circumstances, you can create another reality.

You're not using magic or supernatural powers. Instead, you are simply applying natural laws and power that every person has. It's not something that you can change. It's possible to only change your mind and attitude. This will make your world more interesting and more receptive.

Consider this: If you currently live in a small apartment and desire a larger one, instead of complaining about the financial difficulties and your fate, shift your mindset and envision living in an apartment larger.

It is possible to achieve great things through creative visualization. There are some limitations to the power of visualization. People can be too narrow-minded and don't see beyond their limited circle of influence. They limit their self-worth by what they believe and think. Limit yourself to the things you know. Your potential and opportunities are greater if you're more open-minded than you might be. You are responsible for overcoming any limitations you may have.

What this means is that you have a lot power with your thoughts. How can this be? Let's see.

Creative Visualization Is Very Powerful

*You have probably heard that your thoughts are as important as what they are. This is because images are what people think. Even as you're reading this book, you can see your mind creating mental pictures based on the words. This could be a kiss, ugly divorce, business success or windy day. It is you who actually creates the picture.

*People also create images. Remember the last time you planned something with a friend. Planning requires visualization. Your mind doesn't have a schedule or a spreadsheet. Instead, you use mental movies. You visualize you and your friend doing something.

Images are powerful in manifesting. This power increases when you focus and repeat the process. A single thought, or even a single drop of rain, can make a garden thrive. A combination of powerful emotions and compelling mental images can make your garden thrive.

*Other people may pick up your thoughts without you knowing. The more you are focused and clear in your thoughts, the more people and circumstances will favor you, and the faster your vision will become a reality.

*Imagining an object creates emotions around it. Positive emotions, such as feeling good, are a reward. It is a general rule of thumb that the more you think about your goal and the more positive you feel, the higher your vibration. Soon, you will see the mental emotion/image manifesting in your physical life.

*Creative visualization uses your imagination in order to change your reality. There is no distinction between reality in your actual physical environment and reality in the mind. Only that you have reflexively agreed to one is fake and another is real. These realities are only alternate realities. However, if you concentrate your intentions, they will match the outer reality as well as the inner reality.

*Creative Visualization helps you to overcome limiting beliefs. It's free from any limitations such as money, knowledge or ability. Your concentration on that image will increase and your comfort level in the alternate reality will also increase. It becomes a probability that your thoughts energy continues shaping until it manifests in physical form.

You need to be aware that visualization can only work if you know the right things. These are:

Specificity is key: Uncertainty will send mixed messages.

Listen to what your gut tells you: Only visualize goals that are real to you.

Picture yourself in this vision.

To make your visualization clearer and more realistic, use physical sensations

You can make your visualization more powerful by using positive emotion and great desire

Visualize daily: The duration of the day is not important, but the intensity and consistency of your visualizations.

Remember to be patient. Trees cannot grow overnight. Take the time to notice and appreciate subtle changes that are occurring. These subtle changes can be fun. These changes are a sign of faith.

Positive thinking is key: Keep positive. Be persistent and persistent about this until your old, negative neural pathways become useless.

Chapter 2: The Benefits Of Creative Visualization

You can have many advantages and downsides when you practice creative visualization. Here is a brief list of some of the benefits.

It is something you do every day anyway. There is only one difference: your brain hasn't been taught to use visualization in a way that allows you to get exactly what it wants. It's the difference in eating healthy or eating normal. Everyone has the ability to eat every day. Some people do not understand nutrition, so they are unable to eat healthy meals.

Also, it is important to know the difference between eating only junk food or a balanced, healthy diet. Although junk food can temporarily give you relief, in the long-term you'll feel tired and slow, and may develop other health problems. It is similar with visualization. If you don't train, your mind will be full of junk thoughts. These are negative thoughts that can make it feel like you are not good enough, bad about yourself or lazy. Training will make visualization more effective and empower you.

It produces alpha brainwaves. Creative visualization, at the biological level of your brain, is producing alpha waves. Your brain creates all sorts of waves, depending on your current state. Alpha waves are created when your mind feels relaxed and at ease. These waves can lower blood sugar, reduce anxiety, and regulate your heart rate to reduce your risk of a heart attack.

It is possible to see immediate benefits from creative visualization even before your vision has come to life. Creative visualization can help you shift your mind into alpha waves quickly. You will soon have the mental strength to quickly relax and calm down. That ability can help you eliminate stress and feel overwhelmed almost completely from your everyday life.

It controls your subconscious. The subconscious is responsible in large part for all of our thoughts, feelings, and impulses. Creative visualization allows you to take full control over your subconscious. If you have the ability to control it you will be able to understand yourself better and become more authentic to who you are.

You will also be able reach out to your deepest desires and aspirations. More importantly, you'd be able to identify the reasons why you want them. Your ability to control your impulses can help you understand and manage your emotions.

It's really easy: although it takes practice and patience, creative visualization is great fun. You take the time to envision in vivid detail every aspect your dream life. Creative visualization allows you to imagine how it would feel if you had that life right now. It's a wonderful feeling.

If you feel bored while waiting in line at the pharmacy or at the doctor's, you can take that time to indulge in creative visualization. It's kind of like daydreaming, but with superpowers!

It boosts your confidence. Knowing what you want is key to having confidence. Both of these are possible with creative visualization. Your mind is visualizing every aspect of what you want. You know that your visualizations are becoming more powerful as you get stronger. This will help you to be on your way to achieving your goals. This will boost your confidence. This will help you go a long way in building your confidence.

It can increase the opportunities that you have. This happens for two reasons. Through your positive mental vibrations, creative visualization can help you attract opportunities. Creative visualization can also help you recognize the opportunities that are available to you. This will allow you to be more aware of how everything works together and determine the best way to bring you closer.

Your confidence will allow you to take on more opportunities. Confidence is naturally a magnet for people. People will begin to trust you more and take more chances with you.

It helps to build new neural pathways. Creative visualization can alter your brain structure so you're better equipped for success. Research has shown vividly picturing yourself doing something is as effective as doing it. Imagine yourself playing an athletic sport to train your brain. When you practice for the sport, your mental advantage will be already built. Visualization can be viewed as a form of "mental rehearsal," for real world success.

It reduces anxiety, depression and stress: While increasing your confidence is great, you will also notice a decrease in anxiety and sadness. Creative visualization is responsible for alpha brain wave production, which you already know about. These brain waves will help to reduce anxiety and relax. Creative visualization will increase your confidence and empower you to prevent depression from returning.

It increases your cognitive abilities: creative visualization is actually a mental exercise. It enhances cognitive skills such as focus and concentration, which will allow you to perform better at work, while studying, or playing sports. These are vital skills that you must have to make the most of the opportunities available to you.

These skills will help you to be more confident even if you're still learning. Combine these with the "mental practice" and you will be ready to handle any opportunity that presents itself and reach your goals.

It can help you think more constructively. Instead of dwelling negatively on a problem or thinking that there is nothing you can fix it, you will start to visualize your future after the problem has been resolved. Then, you can go backwards and see what steps you might have taken to overcome the problem.

This allows you to focus on solutions and less on problems. Because your anxiety won't be as high, your ability to solve problems will be greater because you won't feel stressed.

It is a source to inspiration. With these new neural pathways you will actually be more able to make new connections, and come up with innovative ideas that were impossible before.

Your imagination is also growing in detail as you visualize your ideas more clearly. This can lead to more inspiration and new, innovative ideas. This will empower you to create your success stories. You can now use your mental power to achieve success.

Now that you know how creative visualization can benefit your mind, let us look at the types of things creative visualization could help you achieve. The following list does not include all possible uses of creative visualization. Only your imagination can limit the possibilities of creative visualization.

But if this is your first time, it may be difficult to see the purpose of it. There are some guidelines that will help you visualize creatively. This list is intended to encourage you to think deeper about what you really want.

Financial security: This is one of many things that creative visualization can be used to achieve. Jim Carrey used creative visualization, for example to become a millionaire. In 1987, just before his fame, he wrote himself a check for $10,000,000 and dated it for Thanksgiving 1995. He was already signed to a movie contract worth $10 million at the end of 1994.

You can use creative visualization to reach your goals. There are some guidelines you should follow. You don't have to say, "I want rich." Instead, find the specifics.

Jim Carrey did NOT write a check for being rich, but he specified $10 million. He even added "for acting services rendered" to the check. This suggests that he was trying to visualize exactly how much he could earn, how and by what time (1995).

In your creative visualization, make sure you include all these details. The more precise you can visualize, the more powerful the energy that you send to all of the universe. Since like attracts like, it is important to ensure that your positive energy is unique and as specific as possible in order to attract exactly the things that you need to make your creative visualizations come true.

A popular way to use creative visualization is for your career to be more successful at work. It is possible to visualize a promotion or a pay increase, opening your business, starting a company, saving enough for retirement, or other goals. You need to be as precise as possible.

Do you want a raise? Which position would you like promoted to if there is a promotion? What are your responsibilities and the skills that you need to be promoted? You can imagine yourself running a business and leading it to success, if that is what you want.

What is your product/service? How many employees will you need to start? What are the responsibilities of each employee? As the leader and owner of your team, what are your responsibilities? If you are looking to retire comfortably or early, think about how much you will need to save. Think about your lifestyle and the options that you have to help you build your retirement. Are you looking to build it through investing and savings? As you can see, the more details you include in your creative visualization are the better.

To achieve love success, you can also use creative visualization. Imagine yourself meeting your soulmate and restoring your marriage. If you feel it is what your heart desires, you could even visualize yourself getting divorced. It can be as simple as your partner planning the perfect Valentine's date.

It could be something as broad as having a happy family or more specific, like being better at the bedroom. It doesn't matter what you want, but be specific. Imagine you have achieved everything you desire. Visualize yourself together with your soul mate, or in a happy relationship. Add details like what kind of qualities your soulmate has or how you envision a happy marriage. The more detail you provide, the better it will help you to visualize what you want. This can help you understand how to make your dream a reality.

To achieve success in education, you can even use creativity visualization to help you succeed in your studies. Visualize your college of choice and the important final exam. Keep in mind to be as precise as possible and visualize every last detail. The more precise you can make your vision, the more it will come to life.

Specific Objects. Creative visualization doesn't need to be restricted to success, wealth, and other general happenings. You can also use it for everyday life. If you are looking for a new car or a better way to get around, imagine the ideal car. Visualize yourself looking great in a new set of clothes if you are in need of new clothes. What do you envision that outfit looking like?

These types of things can be helped by creative visualization. It is an excellent idea. It is possible to use creative visualization for more things than one. However, don't overcrowd your mind.

One or two creative visualizations is fine, as long you allow yourself to be focused on them and not constantly switch between them.

Chapter 3: How Visualization Can Help You Make Your Plans A Reality

Creative visualization can be described as a mental trick that relies on imagination to bring about one's goals. By using creative visualization you can attract wealth and success. It can help you change your environment, attract wealth and people to your life, and make it happen. Creative visualization is a powerful tool that leads to success.

The possibilities are endless for what you can imagine. Visualization isn't about changing something material. By visualizing, you can change your thoughts and shape your life. The vision board is important because it helps you focus on the right thoughts and make them come true.

The vision board can be described as a simple poster board on which you place images that you have collected. This will help you to remember who you are and where you want it to take you. Here are five ways you can make your own vision board.

Get as many magazines as possible and start to look for images, words, and phrases that appeal to you. You don't have to take it seriously. Let yourself have fun and capture as many images possible.

Now, look through the images in your magazines. This is where to sort your chosen images. This is where you decide which images you want to keep and which you wish to discard. Then you will be able to create a visual board that you envision. Each side of your visualboard may have a different theme, such love.

Love, success and health are the keys to your happiness. You might want to simply place the images or create a book that tells you your story using the images.

Then glue the images that you have selected to your visualboard. You can make it more appealing by being artistic. You can paint the surface or use colored markers to write words.

In the middle of your visionboard, place a picture of you. You should choose a picture in which you feel happy and radiant. This will encourage you to remain positive and help you realize that your dreams can become a reality.

Put your vision board where it is easily visible, so that you can always see it.

Your vision boards will keep you focused on your dreams and inspire you to turn your desires into reality.

There are three types.

I know what my goals are

If you are clear about your goals and desires, this board can help you create a vision board. This could be a house you'd like to buy or a Mercedes Benz.

How to create this board

Make sure to find pictures that reflect your vision. A picture of a Mercedes Benz model or color is a good idea if you are looking for a new car. A grand garden is what you are looking to have in your home.

A picture of your dream home. Cut out images that depict your ideal home if it's a business you want.

Follow these steps to create your vision boards.

Opening and Allowing

If you're not sure what you want, this vision board can help. This is great for people who are just recovering from a time of loss or depression. It is also useful for those who aren't sure what to do or who don't know how. For these people, the "opening to allowing" vision board is the best.

How to make this board

You can go through your magazines and find the photos that make you smile. It doesn't matter whether it's a doll, or a flower. You can have fun choosing images.

Sort through all the images from your magazines. Next, think about what the image means to me. Does the flower signify that I must let go of those who drain my energy? Is the doll important to me? Most likely, you already know the answer. However, if you don't know and still love the picture, pin the image to your visionboard. You will find the answer eventually.

A powerful visualization tool is "opening and accepting" vision boards. It helps you visualize your desires and can also help you discover more about your passion.

Theme

If you are working in a specific area of life like career or work, or you have an important event such as New Year's Eve or your birthday that will start a new cycle, the vision board can help you.

How to create this board

Before you decide on the images that will be displayed on your visionboard, make sure you have a clear picture of the purpose and the theme in your head.

You should choose pictures and images that fit your theme and intention.

The Theme vision Board is unique in that it follows specific parameters and has a clear intent.

If you're feeling adventurous, you might create multiple vision boards. You can start with one type and then change your vision board as your intuition takes you.

Vision boards are an excellent visualization tool. Because the mind cannot distinguish between real and fake, the brain thinks visually. Vision boards can complement your morning rituals and evening practices for gratitude.

You can also use a large sketchbook to create a vision diary that follows the same principles of the vision board. This is especially helpful for those who are going through lots of transitions in their lives.

Chapter 4: Meditation Skills To Help With Visualization

You should first look at the various types of meditation when you are first starting to learn about creative visualization techniques. It can seem confusing to those who have not tried meditation before. It may be confusing to realize that there are many methods you can choose from in order find the one that works best for you. Your mind is as individual as you are, so make sure you look into all options and choose the one that suits you best. Let's explore a few different meditation techniques to get you started on your path towards self-discovery.

Steps to Basic meditation

Get Ready

It is important to have a space that allows you to meditate. Even though you may have difficulties getting into a trance depending on where you sleep, experts suggest that you are most likely to be successful in a seated posture. This is a personal process, so it really comes down where you're most likely to be able to alter your current state. Make sure to be comfortable in the area you choose.

Be comfortable

You should take off your shoes. Also, make sure you aren't wearing any tight clothing. This will allow you to move freely. Comfortable clothes can help you focus when you're struggling to concentrate. To prevent distractions and hunger, it is important that you are not starving. With practice, you'll be able meditation no matter what the world is doing around you. But in the beginning, it will be easier to do so.

Be Free from Distractions

Eliminate as many distractions from your life as you can to help you focus and clear your mind. Your phone should be turned off so that you aren't interrupted. A c.d. You should ensure your c.d. is set up. However, you don't necessarily need it to help you meditate. This can also reduce your abilities as you may become too comfortable with them and not be able get into a trance.

Relax!

Straighten your spine and sit up tall. Begin to relax each part of your body with your eyes closed. Move up from your feet to focus on every muscle and joint. You can continue moving up your entire body. Don't forget to look at your head.

Breathe

You can relax and just focus on your breath. Simply focus on how it feels when the air is inhaled into your lungs and exhaled through your mouth.

A Mantra

You can increase your focus by repeating a simple mantra while you breathe. The mantra could be "breathe into, breathe out". It is vital to not concentrate on what you're saying.

Let Go of Your Thoughts

If you are focusing on the mantra and your breathing, your head will be free from thoughts. Although it may take some time to get used to the routine, you will eventually master it.

Finishing up

Once you are done meditating and ready for the physical world to return, you can count down from 5 while keeping your eyes closed. You can slowly return to your physical awareness by opening your eyes. For quality meditation, you should practice short sessions. You can start with five-minute sessions twice a day and build up from there.

This is not the only method of meditation. There are many other ways to reach the same state of mind.

Breathe.

First, focus on your breathing. This will allow you to enter a meditative mode. This is the first method we'll be looking at.

Choose a comfortable place to sit, such as on the floor or in a chair.

Close your eyes, and bring your tongue to your lips. Breathe only through your nose, while keeping your mouth closed.

Now inhale deeply through the nose. Let the air fill up your abdomen. Next, exhale through your slightly open lips. Focus solely on your breathing while you continue to exhale.

You don't need to think about how you breathe, but instead focus on clearing your thoughts.

Meditation while walking

Although this sounds counterproductive, it is possible to meditate while you walk. This meditation puts your mind on your feet, not your breathing.

When you are walking, just focus on the act of stepping on the ground.

Focus on what is important to you.

Focus on each step, and keep your eyes open.

There are many options for how to get into a meditative state. These are just three possible ways to enter a meditative state. Meditation is only the first step in opening up your awareness. Be patient if you find it difficult to meditate at first. It is normal to take some time to learn how to do it properly and to really enjoy the practice. It is important to keep practicing, so you can reach your ultimate goal.

Chapter 5: Why Do You Need To Incorporate Visualization Into Your Life? What Is The Easiest Way?

Visualization is an effective way to visualize your success. Your success in life will depend on your positive attitude. It will increase self-esteem, confidence, and self-confidence. You can improve your mood by having a positive outlook. This will help to lower the negative effects of your negative thoughts. Below are some tips to help you have a positive attitude.

Open your Mind

To develop a positive attitude and a positive outlook, it is important to be open to hearing the opinions of others. You must understand their perspectives and learn to accept criticisms and suggestions with open minds. For endless possibilities, you can pay attention and be open to their ideas and thoughts.

Write down 10 things you are grateful to God for frequently

On a daily basis, write down 10 things for which you are thankful. It will make you think positively and can help you become more optimistic. It will teach you gratitude for all the good things in your daily life. There's no need to list only the important things. Small things can bring about positive changes in your life.

Learn to Meditate On A Regular Basis

Meditation will allow you to be free from negative thoughts, and it will also help you feel more positive. Meditation can also be used by someone who isn't spiritual. It is important to find a quiet, peaceful place to meditate. To avoid distractions, meditate in a quiet place. Use different meditation techniques to keep your focus on positive things.

To Develop Self-Esteem, Affirmations

To increase self-esteem using Affirmation, you need to focus on your strengths. Focusing on your flaws will not make you stronger. Failures are not what will keep you from being successful. It will help to see you in a more positive light. Below are some affirmations you can use to increase your self-esteem.

My self-esteem keeps increasing on an ongoing basis

- Accepting defeat is okay. Let's focus on the good aspects.
- I have faith in my abilities
- I can do any thing
- My self-confidence is high.
- Everything I want is possible
- I love and trust me

- I have confidence in my abilities
- Positive thoughts of me are what I can speak.
- I am beautiful and creative
- Find Negative Thoughts & Fears to kill them

As the first step, ask yourself: Do you have negative or positive thoughts most of the time? This is where you need to identify negative thought patterns. Negative thoughts begin with:

"Can't do" should be replaced with "can".

It is better to say "No" than "Yes".

Instead of being confident, be less confident

Success instead of failure

If these thoughts are ingrained in your brain, it is feeding negativity. Captivation of people through their thoughts is the greatest problem of our era. It is easy to let your thoughts control your life instead of using them for your good. It is essential that you learn to control your thoughts.

Untapped Tools to Power Your Mind

Mental strength can be important for coping with many problems and complications in life. The following five points are common, but they are often overlooked.

Confidence is the key to belief

You can overcome any adversity

Capacity to bear pain

Desire and determination for your next step

Ability to overcome fear

Confidence

Confidence is the cornerstone of mental strength. It can help you achieve your goals in any sport. Confidence is essential to be able to reach your goals. If you think you aren't capable of achieving your goals, you will likely fail and not be able move on. Positive influences can undermine your confidence and increase self doubt. You must believe that you are capable of achieving your goals.

Overcome Adversity

There are times when everyone will face hardship. You might find it difficult to manage injuries, family issues, and professional or personal commitments. You need to have the confidence and ability to deal with hardships.

It is important to be positive in all situations. These kinds of situations are a great way to filter out selfish and ineffective people. Keep in mind that these situations are not hopeless and you can endure them.

Tolerate Pain

Your life will be filled with pain. Because this will allow you to achieve new heights of success, it is important to be able to accept pain. You often find success hidden behind difficulties and hardships. You can learn to live with pain and increase your ability to handle it. You will be able to confront any negative or unexpected event in your life with courage.

Stop living in a negative environment

Take a look around to see who is generating negative energy. There are many people in your life who will share negative energy with you. These people have the right to take over your thoughts. You must manage everything and eliminate these people from your daily life. Change your location if you have any unpleasant memories. All those who know such things or can repeat them in your life should be removed. It is important to distance yourself from these people and create a new circle.

Chapter 6: Visualization Techniques

There are three main ways to visualize that you can use every day to help you achieve your short- and long-term goals. These techniques are vision boards and meditation. Creative visualization is the most important topic I covered. However, I'm going in detail to show you what it is and how it can be used to improve your life.

Vision board

What is it?

A vision board is a collection of images taken from magazines or books. These images are then glued to a poster so that you can remember what you want. Place the poster where you will see it every day. The idea behind this technique, is to surround yourself in images and things you love to make your subconscious want those things.

A few materials are required to create a visionboard.

Poster board

Images of the things you are looking for in life. To keep your interest going, make sure you have several options.

Glue

Before you start creating your vision boards, take a moment to consider what it is you are looking for. You can also meditate on what it is you desire to achieve in your life.

Tip: If the majority of your time is spent on the computer, it might make sense to create a virtual image board that can be used as your background. I spend most my day on my laptop. So, I created a collage that contains images that represent my goals and dreams. It gives me an instant boost when I feel unproductive or down about something.

How it works

Before I go on about creating your visionboard, I will explain the psychology behind the process. Studies have been done with both control groups and those who were given images to view. Before the group of business decision-makers was asked for their opinions, they were given nothing to view. They made most of their business decisions based on logic reasoning or past experiences. The second group was provided with images of money to view before they were asked questions. The second group was only able to make financial decisions.

The moral of this story is to use logic if you are trying to achieve something. Use pictures that are more logical. Post pictures of happy couples or other images that inspire loving feelings if you are trying to achieve emotional things, such as love.

Let's now examine the five steps required to create a vision board that can be used for visualization techniques.

Step One

Find your images. Images should speak to you. Pick the images that best represent the emotions you are trying to stir. You can make a list of phrases, words and images from all your sources.

Step Two

This is the time to use your intuition. Simply lay out the images you find most meaningful on the board. This is where the final step of culling the herd. Get rid of images that don't feel right to you. You might have more than one goal for your board. If so, you can group the images by what they are related to. To tell a story, you could fold the board into book form.

Step Three

Attach all of your images to the board. You have two options: you can add text to caption your images, or you can let them speak for themselves.

Step Four

You don't need to do this step if it makes you feel self-conscious. However, it would be smart to leave a spot at the middle of the board and to put a photo of you looking radiant and happy there.

Step Five

It's a good idea to place the visionboard somewhere you see often. If you've created a vision board, you can keep it on your mobile phone, computer desktop, or wherever else electronic. Even better, take a photograph of your vision board at work and keep it with you in your purse or wallet.

Three Vision Boards

There are three kinds of vision boards you have the option to make. All relate to your personal goals. I will be asking you a series questions. Based on your answers, you'll decide which board to create.

Are you clear about your goals and desires? Y/N

Do you desire to change your environment? Y/N

Is there anything you want to manifest like a new car, or a home? Y/N

Don't you know exactly what it is you want? Y/N

Did you ever experience depression or grief? Y/N

Is it difficult to know what vision you are looking for? Y/N

Do you know that you would like some type of change but aren't certain if it's possible or not? Y/N

Is it a particular season, like a New Year's resolution, birthday wish, or other such thing? Y/N

Are you focused on one aspect of your personal life, such relationship or career? Y/N

If you answered "Yes" to questions one through three you should create a 'I Know What I want' vision board. If you answered yes on questions four through seven, then you need to create an Open and Allowing' visionboard. If you answered yes either of these questions, then you should create a theme vision board.

Vision Board "I know What You Want"

This vision board is focused on a specific dream or goal that you have in your mind. This is why you should include images that reflect your desired goal, such a home near water or opening a bakery.

Vision Board - "Open and Allowing"

The vision board is ideal for people who don't know what they want, but are clear about their goals. This vision board is perfect for people looking to improve their self-esteem, confidence, happiness, and overall well-being. Just go through all your images and look for the ones that make you happy. Pick images that you feel drawn to, even if it's not obvious why. This will help you to understand what it all means.

Vision Board: 'Theme'

Vision boards have a clear goal. For example, a vision board may help you lose weight or get promoted. To create your vision boards, first make sure you have a clear picture in your mind of what you want. Choose images that correspond to that theme only.

Meditation

What it is

Before I go into detail about meditation, let me first explain what it isn't.

Meditation isn't a losing of control, a mental exercise or a loss. It is a state that allows you to be in a constant state of awareness and inner peace. This state can be very hard to reach and requires lots of practice. Even monks need to meditate for years in order to reach this state.

It works

It has been proved that meditation can work. An MRI scan of Buddhist monks revealed that their brain waves had changed during meditation. When they were in meditation, the monks reached a Delta state of mind. To help you understand this further, I will briefly discuss the various brain wave patterns.

Gamma

Gamma state refers to hyperactivity. It is when we try to learn something extremely difficult or feel an adrenaline rush. A woman trying save her child would be experiencing gamma thoughts. If we live in this state of mind, we become constantly anxious.

Beta

The beta state, where we are not actively thinking for long periods of time, is the most relaxed state of mind. This is a alert state in which we are actively learning, planning, assessing and categorizing information.

Alpha

The alpha is when we are slowing down. You will feel more grounded and calm in this state. This is where most students are after a yoga session or when they're getting ready to go to bed.

Theta

The most popular place to meditate is in theta. This is the mental state where the verbal brain moves into the visible mind. This is commonly described as a "drowsy" state of mind, where the mental process shifts from planning to deeper awareness. In this state, visualization is possible.

Delta

The ultimate state of mind Tibetan monks are well-known for is the Delta state. This is where the human brain is still awake, but has stopped processing information. It simply is being. A normal person can achieve this state of mind in deep, dreamless sleeping.

How to meditate

Meditation is easy. Simply focus on your breath to transition from the beta/alpha state to theta. The mind and breath work together so when your breath slows down or lengthens, your brainwaves will slow down or increase. Tibetan monks, who are in a meditation state or the delta pattern, will not need to breathe as often while they are meditating.

Start meditation by laying down on the floor or in your chair. Then, focus on your breath and sit back. Place your hands on the floor and relax your shoulders. Close your eyes, and place your hands in the lap.

Be aware of how your body is moving. Do not try to control it. Instead, observe it. Pay attention.

You can silently repeat to your self that you are taking in air and taking out. Don't be afraid to let your mind wander.

It is best to meditate early in the morning and late at night. For five minutes each day, it will be enough.

Creative Visualization

What It Is

It is the art of creating a picture or scenario that represents your goals. Imagine what you would like to accomplish in your life. Then picture yourself doing it. It is important to spend at least five minute a day visualizing your goals and picturing them in detail. As you do this, make sure to use all of your senses. To be able run a marathon within a given time frame, it is important to smell the water, feel the cool air on your skin, and enjoy the company of other runners.

It is important to imagine yourself in this position. See yourself achieving this goal through your own eyes, and not through those of others. You can add color to the visuals and even some background music. Make it vivid and big.

You can visualize the goal by physically acting it out. Do not just visualize the house you wish to buy. Visualize how you will go about signing the paperwork, inserting your key into the front door, hosting your house warming party.

Try to imagine what it would look like if someone else has achieved it. This will give your brain visual cues that will help it visualize what it will look like once you accomplish your goal.

It works

Our subconscious mind will act on the thoughts we repeat every day if they are repeated repeatedly. Habits and behaviors can be formed by this process. These habits and behaviors will eventually lead to success in our lives. Each thought can bring about an emotion, and if the emotion is strong enough we will be compelled to act.

Chapter 7: The Commitment

You are therefore urged, brethren to offer your bodies as a holy and living sacrifice to God. This will be your spiritual service of worship. (Romans 12:1-2)

Next after visualization, comes commitment. You must dedicate yourself to the attainment of your dreams and goals. We've already seen how to get the fuel we need for this. Now let's find out how we can make it more efficient and friendly towards achieving our true desires and goals.

In his works, Daniel Kahneman, the renowned psychologist, talks about two distinct parts in our minds. He names these, according to Kahneman's terminology, the remembering self or the experiencing self. Kahneman explained that the recalling self is responsible in part for our memories, and for recollection events that are meaningful. This is what resonates with progress within us. However, the experiencing self is responsible in part for immediate pleasures. While the first is more likely to have a retrospective quality, it stems from a judgement that we have made, the second relates to our immediate sense reactions, which make up the current moment. Both of these elements can never be separated. This is illustrated by the fact that a choice made in the present by the experiencing person may lead to the remembering one later. Let's say a person smokes. The person might smoke a cigarette and enjoy the immediate pleasure that nicotine gives her. However, she may also cough up the harmful tar from the cigarettes, which could lead to her concluding that smoking is a bad habit.

We'll be focusing on how we remember ourselves and how that relates to our obligations, both in front of God and our selves. It gives you a sense that we are unique, it gives you stability, and it also gives you the upper hand with respect to your counter-part. To live a mindful life where we fulfil our dreams and that others can benefit, is to live a happy, fulfilling life.

The only way to make a commitment is to use our God-endowed intellect and choose ways that are beyond base, instinctual feelings. These choices transcend boredom and passive, subconscious pain. Kahneman's selves were chosen because they best reflect our human nature. It is divine and sinful. Sometimes we neglect ourselves, lose authorship of our own stories, and so we fall into the traps that sorrow and sin can cause, choosing to be unhappy and choosing to focus on our weaknesses rather than our strengths.

Visualize yourself as strong and driven towards fulfillment. Remember your commitment to your goal every time a distraction comes into your day, or vice attempts to manifest itself through your life. This is the considered living I'm talking about. It's how you take back control of your own life. This is how God can make you happy.

By focusing on the long-term benefits that you will enjoy over the course your life, you can engage in more of the activities that make yourself a better individual. The dome of commitment encompasses your values and intentions as well as your actions. To achieve the results that you are meant to reach, it is important to have healthy passions, desires, and goals that drive you to your core.

Instead of falling prey to your sinful and animal instincts and settling for the status quo, strive to achieve your highest goals and keep your purpose in life alive. Your life should be filled with excellence. Faith is a quality that is built in you. Once it is beautifully visualized through speculative desires, it will naturally spring forth through your deeds. You can cultivate your own wisdom and knowledge by using the techniques you have already learned. Be aware of false desires and urges.

You must be willing to let go of your bestial nature in order to commit to your goals. Your faith in God will allow you to write your own story and your actions will help you reach your goals. Congruence is when there is always congruence between one's intention, thoughts, or actions.

Never forget that there is no quick route or shortcut to success. To be successful, you must not cheat or divert from the strategies we discussed earlier. You will reap what is sown; have faith in the purpose of your life and never lose sight of it. Always smile and look forward to the next challenge God places before you.

Chapter 8: Uncovering Your Creativity With Auto-Suggestion

Your creativity can be revealed by learning how to use auto-suggestion. But what is auto-suggestion exactly?

Auto suggestion can also refer to speech and thoughts. It can refer to any of the five sensory senses. If you just want to take a bite of fresh baked muffins from a bakery, you're automatically suggesting that you feel hungry. It's a way of subconsciously communicating. You can influence your entire mind by controlling the thoughts that are subconsciously entered into your mind.

This is what auto-suggestion really is. Your conscious brain is the gatekeeper. The conscious mind is responsible for allowing thoughts to enter the subconscious. The conscious mind is able to either stop a bad idea from coming about or make a positive decision. Individuals have complete control over any thoughts that they allow to enter their subconscious via any one of the five senses. However, most people do not exercise this control. People who fail to exercise control can get stuck in a rut and never achieve their goals.

For a simpler explanation, think about the difference between good and bad food. You can choose the foods you put into your body. Bad food can ruin your health and cause a host of diseases. Or, you could choose to eat well and live a happy, healthy life. The same goes for your mind. You can consciously choose to allow good thoughts or to reject them. This is what auto-suggest is all about.

You were instructed previously to write down your "statements for success", what you most desire, and then to repeat them to yourself. Doing this will help you communicate what you desire to your subconscious. This is what cultivates trust.

Repetitionly reading your goals aloud is a way to create positive habits for yourself and your mind.

Keep in mind that you can't read the entire statement you made without thinking. This will have little effect. You can think of an actor reading lines. Are you inspired or influenced by the actor reading their lines in a monotone voice, with a solemn expression? Or, are you inspired more by the actor who puts feelings into their lines?

For most people, it should be the last.

The same applies to your statement. It's not possible to make it a habit that you do all day. When you read the text, you need to be conscious of your thoughts and emotions. Do not just read the text. Take the time to really read the goals and feel the emotion associated with achieving them.

Why?

Because it will bring you better results. Study after study has shown that the best way to improve your results at the gym is to think about the muscles. Yoga is an effective exercise because it focuses on the area that you want to improve. This technique does not serve only the body. It works for the brain. For the best results and outcomes, you need to be able to focus on what you want.

As you have faith that your workout will improve your body, your mind will be helped if you speak your thoughts aloud.

Remember, there is no such thing a "thing for nothing." It is important to work in order to succeed. Work hard and push yourself to grow your muscles. If you want to succeed, you have to push yourself and strive for your goals. Daily readings are the first step.

It is important to be able 100% to focus on what you want. Concentration is what will convert a passing desire to a burning need, something that takes control of your thoughts. This ability is directly related with your ability and ability to use autosuggestion.

Concentration is the only way you can use the 6 steps from chapter 2 effectively. Concentration starts with deciding how much money you really need. Remember that trip to Italy? She needed a precise amount. She focused on that number and could see it appear with her eyes closed. This is where it's at all times. This is what must be done every day.

Your imagination is your best friend. You will see the possibilities for what you can do to get the money you desire or the item of your dreams. Do not wait for a plan to be made. When you can see yourself spending money, you must put the plan into action. Although the plan may appear quickly, it might be only a flash of your mind. But, you have to grab that plan in your mind and put it into action.

Keep these steps in mind:

First, find a quiet area where you can close the eyes and repeat what you wrote. You need to be able to repeat the written statement without being interrupted. If you close your eye, you must see yourself in possession your goal.

Second, repeat the process every morning and at night until you can actually see the money in front of you when you close you eyes.

Third: Make sure you keep a printed copy of the goals in front of you so that it never slips from your mind.

You are initiating auto-suggestion. Your subconscious will only respond to instructions you believe in.

No matter how difficult or confusing these instructions seem, it is vital that you adhere to them. You will soon learn how powerful these rules are and can achieve the success which you desire.

Many people believe they control their destiny. How can this be true? You have the power and ability to influence your subconscious mind to create any kind of change in your life.

Auto-suggestions can only be made conscious. Therefore, it is important to make conscious efforts to follow the guidelines. Remember that these guidelines will guide you to success.

Chapter 9: Lucid Dreaming; The Practicalities

There are many scientific facts you should know about dreams and sleep before you learn how to Lucid Dream. This chapter will cover the basics and types of Lucid Dreams that you can expect as you use the steps we describe later in this book.

False Awakening

This is often referred to as Lucid Dreaming but it is not. This dream involves the individual "awaking" to find themselves in a room similar to or the same as the one in which he/she expected to be (the bed they slept in). They often start their morning routine and then wake up to see if it is a false awakening. Only then does consciousness kick in, and the individual will realize they were dreaming.

Sleep Paralysis

Again, this condition can be confused with Lucid Dreaming. However it is usually experienced in a half-awake state. When we are asleep, our bodies become paralyzed. This is a method of self-protection that stops us from physically acting out what we dream. This happens in normal sleep, normal sleeping and Lucid Dreaming. The individual may feel as though they can't move, or even experience "hypnagogic", hallucinations. These uncontrolled visions and sounds can be caused by our subconscious. Hearing someone calling your name is a common auditory hallucination. Lucid Dreaming practitioners often report an increase in the incidence of sleep paralysis. In this condition, you may experience awaking from sleep while still in this state. This can seem disturbing at first. Paralysis and the sounds/images are normal body functions and should not cause concern.

Prompting Lucid Dreams

There are three general ways we can enter the Lucid Dream. These are:

Dream Initiation of Lucid Dreams

Mnemonic initiation of Lucid Nights (MILD).

Waking initiation of Lucid Dreams

DILD

This is the most natural and common way Lucid Dreams happen. The dreamer falls asleep and begins to dream. The dreamer awakens from a dream by the unconscious part of their brain, or parts thereof. These dreams often have a mundane aspect. The events of the dreams will occur every day, or they will not be unusual. You may find some aspects of the dream strange, or you may have never experienced them before. The dreamer begins to feel control over their dreams and can influence the events. This Lucid Dream type is what most people will experience. However, there aren't any proven methods to make it happen. Although it will happen at any stage of your life, this is the most natural form.

MILD

Stephen LaBerge, an expert in Lucid Dreaming, pioneered this technique. This technique works by training your mind to recognize that it is dreaming. This is surprisingly easy. This is done by creating a habit that you can continue while you sleep, and then continuing the habit when you wake up. You should recognize the activity as a sign you are dreaming. Although this sounds complicated, it's really quite easy. Some suggestions include counting your fingers whenever you are awake, but preferably before bed. You can look at each one and make a mental image. After counting and staring at each finger for a few moments, relax and you will fall asleep. After falling asleep, the brain begins to order and analyze the day's events. It might get to the end first. This method is generally successful. You must consider your visual perception. The fingers in your dream may seem to be more many than they really are or might be missing. This is your cue that you are dreaming. Realizing this realization is the moment when parts of your subconscious mind are reactivated. From here, you can start to control your dream. The MILD method is especially helpful for beginners. You can start using it in days or weeks.

WILD

This technique can be more difficult than MILD, and it may take practice to master. The DILD and MILD techniques to initiate Lucid Dreaming see the individual fall asleep normally, dream and then a part of their consciousness turns back on. You can use this technique to "keep your consciousness switched on" when you fall asleep, and then enter into a dream mode. You can achieve this by using relaxation techniques and meditation. The idea is to just fall asleep with your conscious mind partially focused. This technique is especially useful at certain points during the sleep cycle. If REM's is interrupted, it will start again immediately when you fall asleep. It is possible to induce dreaming by getting up earlier than usual or taking a break from work. It is possible to enter a Lucid

Dream by combining this technique with a relaxation strategy to get your body to sleep quickly.

Note: This technique is most likely to cause sleep paralysis, or a loss of movement when you fall asleep. You might experience loss of motion, a feeling of falling, or strange visions and sounds. This is normal. It happens every time we go to sleep. You should be ready for some odd experiences if you try this method.

Chapter 10: Visualization Techniques & Exercises You Should Be Knowledgeable

It's not just about imagination. Most of us start at the goal and get stuck there. Sometimes we have good intentions and sometimes a strategy, but we can't seem making it happen. Aristotle outlined the three stages of achieving your dreams in these three stages. You can then adjust your resources to meet that end.

The two methods for positive visualization are

Outcome Visualization;

This is the first step toward making positive visualization a reality. This is what most people find very helpful.

Process visualization

This requires you to envision all the actions that are necessary for you achieve your goals.

These simple steps can help you have a more positive visualisation

Don't let your guard down. Your chances of success in life are not going to change if you feel bad about yourself. Positive mentality will enable you to see the possibilities and will eventually accomplish them. If you don't think it will, then it probably won't work. The first step to effective visualization of the impossible is positive thinking.

Once you've taken the time to visualize your goals in detail, you need to transfer them to the real world. Prior to focusing on the activities that will allow you to achieve those goals, however small or large they may seem, FOCUS.

Take a moment, slow and steady wins the race. Visualization works best when you are calm, relaxed, and not worrying. This technique is also known as meditation, hypnosis, or hypnosis. It's just more active, vivid, real and effective. Focusing more will make you more focused, even if distractions are minimal.

To be successful, you must fit into the personality of the person you are trying to become. You will discover the many skills you need to be more successful.

Be honest about it. Although pictures, drawings, painting and painting may be cool, there is power in the tongue. If you see your dream car passing by, think of it as your car. Make sure you have plans and a concrete plan to get it.

Keep your expectations realistic and don't be afraid to push yourself beyond your comfort zone. For example, if you dream of being a boxer, but you want to beat legendary wrestlers like John Cena or Batista Kane, you should wake up. You are not that great, so you must work hard and continue training. This is how you can overcome any obstacle.

These visualization exercises could also be useful

- Take a photograph of you in ten year's time, look at the photo, then drop and try your best to visualize it

- Look at a 3D object. If possible, feel it. After that, picture the book.

- View these images in real life

- You can imagine yourself in the real environment.

Expect results

Chapter 11: My Secret To Happiness

Happiness can be described as the feeling people want to experience but are unable to achieve. Some people experience happiness for a short time, but it is not something they can sustain long-term. People have a common misconception about the law. They think that if they focus only on the future they will get what is best for them. I have so many clients who I share the law if attraction with. They don't use it at all, then just next week they tell me that it doesn't work.

If you find that focusing on tomorrow makes you anxious, then this strategy is not for you. You should feel like a millionaire right away and that feeling all day. It's about not imagining it in the morning, and then throughout the day having a poor mindset and wondering why it's not happening. This is what I used too. I was so stressed about not having what I wanted. I would blame the book I was reading and then say that it doesn't work. There is a time when you will achieve what you desire.

The magic happens when your life and actions become the person you want. You don't need to be surrounded by external objects; all you want is the sensation of being able to feel it. You don't need to be financially free to feel secure. However, you can experience that feeling of security immediately. You might be tempted to say that you need to see the money to believe it, but this is why you must take two steps forward. I did this for a whole year and didn't get what I wanted, but I kept trying and failing. I realized that I wasn't getting what was expected of me because I was living in a broken mindset. I was looking forward to the future with all my heart and only focusing on it.

Write down the following: "I'm so lucky that I have my partner of dreams, the financial security of my car, the house and the house that are mine." You need to be passionate about your desire and talk about it passionately. It will attract it quicker.

I used to wake up every morning and visualise my perfect life for ten minutes. Then I would go into the shower thinking it was Fijian and my brain would believe it. Do something different, think differently about your life and say "Thank you" for being successful.

What would your dream self sound like? How would he/she walk and communicate with people? How much more confident would you have? If you want to feel more confident, you should write now. It will not happen. You'll have the same mindset and you won't feel fulfilled. I used to imagine that one day, I would feel confident, be with the right person, and be happy when I made a certain amount. But the problem was, I kept thinking I would one day be happy if everything was achieved.

Imagine yourself wasting a decade in hopes that you will one day feel fulfilled. You can be happy now, no matter your current financial position. Some people are in financial distress. I've been there and I understand the stress and frustration that it can cause. I used be anxious all the time. I would worry about how I was going get my rent, food, and bills paid. It makes it feel bad and you start to feel the same way every day. I told myself I was financially secure and had more than enough. This was how I got out of my poverty mindset. This is how you get incredible ideas. It was the way I got my first business idea. This is the law behind attraction and it's why you should trust your ideas.

I trusted the idea that I received, and I have never regretted it. I was grateful for the opportunity to be able to feel happy when it became stressful. Be the person you wish to be, and start living that way. Start the day with a smile on your face and focus on the things you love in your life. This will make the law of attraction work for your favor. Change your negative thoughts for positive ones and realize that all you have in life is yours to attract. It is possible to see the future in the present moment and the past is connected to it. Realize that making a choice now to feel happy will send a vibration through the universe to make you feel happier, which will attract happiness to others.

Chapter 12: Unleashing The Amazing Power Of Meditation And How It Can Literally Help Your Brain Explode With Creativity

Once you have achieved your focus, it is now time to put your brain into action. Meditation helps you achieve greater clarity and insight. Guess what? Clearness of vision and purpose, along with good insight, can lead to significant breakthroughs and innovative ideas.

How can you unlock the amazing power of meditation to inspire you to be more creative? These are easy and fun tips that will allow you to unleash the creative power of meditation.

1. Make a mess.

Hurry! Grab the best art material that you can. Anything! Grab hold of them and get squiggling! After meditation, your brain will feel calm and relaxed. Making a mess with any material can help you unleash your creativity potentials. Creativity is about self-expression. Use your fingers to paint, or use other objects as paintbrushes. Do whatever you want, and have fun messing around. You'll find that your stress levels drop dramatically and you feel more motivated.

2. Write down your insights.

Do not worry about the grammar. Once you are done meditating, write whatever comes to your mind. It's possible to be surprised by the amazing advice and plot hooks that your creative muse or idea dragon has provided.

Write down everything you think and then read it aloud. What you will hear is the idea, the inventions, or the inspiration that have been hidden within your mind, but blocked by fear, doubt, and worries.

3. Goodbye, Anxiety

It's true. Regular meditation sessions calm the mind and lower the likelihood of anxiety attacks. What does all this have to do creativity?

Simply put, less worry = more creativity. Less anxiety = more productivity. It is easier to focus on the task at hand when you are less anxious about what you must accomplish for the day. You are able handle every task with confidence, clarity and decisiveness. With your calmed and clear mind, you can increase your productivity by reviewing your to-do list, and then deciding, without fear, that you will complete your tasks by end of day.

4. Enjoy the creative process.

You can't beat the feeling of being creative, whether you are a painter, sculptor or actor. But what does this really mean? How can you lose yourself in meditation?

Did you ever realize that creativity can come anywhere? Meditation falls under the umbrella of "virtually anyplace." It is more likely that your next great idea will come to you after your meditation session.

Make it a habit. When you are calm and have meditated, go ahead and do whatever you enjoy doing. Go wild with it. If you are a writer, let the words guide your writing instead of the opposite. Let yourself be engrossed in the intricate details of any plot and characters you've ever considered but were too scared or afraid to create. If you are an artist, you can let the colors you thought would never work together free you. Engineers and doctors alike can get lost in the creative process. Explore, experiment! Dare to try something completely new. You'll find that meditation is crucial in allowing your intuitions and senses to prevail over your fears, pressures, and doubts.

Chapter 13: Relaxed Mind By Reaching Alpha Brainwaves

It is essential to master how to be deeply relaxed in mind as well as body to make your dreams a reality. Alpha brainwaves are achieved when you relax or do nothing that requires much thought. For example, if you're just relaxing on a couch and watching television, then this is alpha brainwaves. The "relaxingwaves" are alpha waves. Because the alpha brainwaves act as a bridge to your subconscious mind (theta), they are vital. If you didn't have the alpha brainwaves in your brain, there wouldn't be any bridge to deep thought, feelings, memories or creativity.

Certain frequencies of alpha frequency have very significant effects on the human brain and body. A series of Youtube videos can be listened to in order to increase alpha waves. They are scientifically called binaural beatings. There are two binaural beats, each with a specific amplitude. After that there is a brain-generated third beat which is the one between the two first beats. The brain will tune into the frequency by assimilating the third tonal. For example, if the first beat had 220Hz and then the second was at 210Hz, then 10Hz would be the third created beat.

Different Alpha Frequencies.

8.5Hz: There are no studies that show any particular effects at this frequency.

9Hz- This is associated with Sacral Chakra. It helps to balance the body and alerts to any imbalances.

9.5Hz is where you will find the bridge between your subconscious mind (theta), as well as the conscious mind(beta).

10Hz - It has been proven to be helpful in treating jet lag or a hangover.

10.5Hz- Lowers blood Pressure, Improves Immunity, Ability to Achieve Freedom, Activity, and Energy

11Hz- Will achieve a relaxed, alert state of mind

11.5Hz- is associated to increased mental efficiency.

12Hz- refers to the throat chakra. This is where all other frequencies can be experienced mental clarity.

You can increase your Alpha Waves. There are several techniques that can be used to boost your alpha brainwaves.

You can learn how to increase your alpha brainwaves by listening to guided fantasy meditation. You can find several of these videos on YouTube. They feature a calm voice that tells you what image to create. To vividly visualise the image they wish you to see, use all your senses.

You can imagine your day in the early morning or during your morning bath, with calm and relaxed thoughts.

By listening to binaural beats, you can increase your alpha brainwaves by increasing your frequency of binaural beats.

Alpha Brainwaves & Meditation. The results of meditation that is non-directive tend to show more significant changes in the alpha brainwaves activity. This method yields better results than resting and not using any mental techniques.

Alpha Brainwaves are used in visualization exercises. The use of Alpha brainwaves in visualization exercises is a good idea. These waves are created when you are not awake and completely relaxed in the occipital. The occipital brainlobe, which is the area where visual images are processed, is located in the brain. Alpha waves are created here and oscillate in 8-13Hz cycles per second and can be measured using an electroencephalography (EEG). The alpha state is when your brain has slowed. Your brainwaves oscillate with a higher frequency during consciousness. The brain's visual performance becomes stronger when it produces lower frequency waves when we are barely awake and relaxed.

Shifting into Alpha. Relax, close your eyes, and slowly slow your breathing into a rhythmic pattern. This is one of the best ways to get your mind to shift to Alpha. You should inhale through you nose and exhale from your mouth, keeping both equally balanced. To put it another way, you need to exhale the same amount of air as you inhaled. You can check that your diaphragm has been relaxed by releasing your stomach slightly so it protrudes a little. Next, slowly pull it in until your stomach touches your spine. Do this exercise every day to reach alpha. Although it may feel awkward at first, you will soon find that the difficulty will disappear. This is a great exercise to help relieve all tension. You must focus on your breath. This level of focus can be hard due to natural distractions like thoughts. These skills require practice, concentration, as well as commitment.

As you reach alpha and continue to work towards it, it is crucial that you keep your mind free from outside thoughts. It is difficult work. Try to keep this exercise going for at least 2 to 3 seconds when you start. Gradually, increase the time. You'll eventually develop a rhythm that suits your needs and focus will naturally come to you. If you can spend five minutes doing this exercise, you're probably doing a great job in getting your brainwaves into alpha. Once you achieve this, your mind will begin to draw more energy form the occipital-lobe. The alpha waves of energy that are generated by the visualization techniques that you choose will be carried along with your experience. This will make it intense and powerful.

Chapter 14: Butterfly Visualization

Allow your body and mind to relax. Your arms can rest on either your sides, or your heart chakra folded. Comfortable clothes are important.

Close your eyes and enjoy the moment. It is important to let go of all thoughts and silence your mind. If you have any, let them in and they will roll away as waves that gently approach the lakeshore.

Waves gradually come in and slowly go out. Every thought must move with the tides. Every emotion must move forward and backward.

Take some time to relax and enjoy the moment. You are free to be where you want to be. You don't have to be anywhere at this time. There is nothing that you need to do at the moment.

It is possible for your mind to wander off into other thoughts. However, you should keep your eyes focused on the present moment.

Breathe deeply. Breathe deeply and inhale positive energy. Breathe love energy. Inhale negative energy, and exhale anger. Repeat the process three to five consecutive times.

Imagine yourself in a calm, peaceful place. You're now in a secure place that no one can ever harm you. It is your place.

You don't have to think about what you should do or not do. You can be yourself. Allow the experience itself to flow naturally. You can breathe at your own pace.

As you stroll through the garden, you will see monarch butterflies balance themselves on a variety of flowers. It is amazing to see them delicately flutter their wings.

Let yourself fly. Let your imagination fly and pursue your dreams. Watch your heart beat slow down as their wings move softly up and back. With their tiny legs, they hop from petal to petal.

The leaves glow in the sunlight and look so green. Butterflies balance on the most delicate stems while drinking nectar. They do this by giving a light kiss.

All the old baggage is gone. Feel light and free of all the burdens in your life. Allow yourself to be full of color, radiate love everywhere you go.

Simple living is the best thing. Let go of all the troubles. Stop trying to make things work. Keep your eyes on the present and take in what is happening. Allow your soul and spirit to awaken. Enjoy a calm mind.

Fly in the wind and feel the summer breeze. Enjoy the sweet scent of lavender & lilac perfume in the air. Listen to nature's best friends buzz, chirp or tweet a beautiful tune.

You will notice a change in your body as you release the heaviness and weight that is holding you down. Breathe in slowly and calmly. Your legs and arms will relax. Enjoy the feeling of relaxation as you take a break in this lovely garden of love.

As monarchs dance from flower to flower in the garden, rainbows of color bloom all around it. Life is like a dance. It's a wonderful way to relax and enjoy a peaceful life. Let your wings fly and let the flowers take you to your personal song.

Keep this feeling going for as long and as you want. If you are ready to stop the meditation, you can at any time.

Close your eyes. Let your mind drift off for a while and then let it settle.

Chapter 15: How To Make Visualization Work For You

Visualization is an effective way to train your mind. Visualization is like a treadmill that you use to improve your thinking, basically whipping them into shape. Visualization is a great tool for improving your outlook on life and helping you overcome fears of public speaking. You can worry about or think about something in your life that is bothering you, as well as a potential undesirable outcome. However, it's just as easy to visualize something you love and a wonderful outcome.

It is unfortunately more common to focus on the negative for many people.

Visualization, in a nutshell is like daydreaming about the beautiful dream you choose, but at the right time and place. It's similar to daydreaming about the outcome that you desire. It's your duty to make this a habit, using the examples in this book and your own. This allows you to tailor the visualizations to suit your individual needs. It is always best that you find a quiet area where you will not have to be disturbed for at minimum ten minutes. The more you do it, the more effective it will be.

It doesn't matter whether you read visualizations from the book, listen or create guided visualizations. Whatever your choice, keep the same time and place every day. It doesn't make a difference where you go, so long it is quiet and unperturbed for at most 10 minutes. It is okay that life happens. Do not let it get you down if you are late for a day or two. You can always get back on your horse again and start over. You will see visible results in the shortest amount of time if you do it every day or more often than that. If this is not possible try to aim for at most three times per week.

It is better to be rested and alert before you start to visualize. Not the best time to visualize is at the end a long and stressful day.

If you are looking for a quick boost of energy to allow you to focus on the important things and not lose your mind, there are a few tricks that may help. These include: a cup green tea or coffee, vitamins or fruit drinks, and energy drinks.

It is possible to practice just a few times per day, but it will still be beneficial if it becomes a routine. There is no wrong or right way to do this, so long as it is done with regularity. It will pay off. However, the more you do this, the more positive changes you will experience in your thinking and your life.

Your inner world will be more happy and peaceful as your outer world.

You won't change your life overnight. As you embark on this journey, you'll notice changes.

The Consciousness & the Subconscious

The Conscious mind

Your conscious mind refers to the part of your mental system that is responsible for reasoning and logic. If I asked for you to multiply 2x6 times 6, it would be your conscious brain that would calculate and arrive in twelve.

You can also control every action you take intentionally while conscious. Your conscious mind decides whether you want to drink a cup of tea, or coffee. If you are conscious of something that you do, you can be sure it is because of your conscious brain.

The conscious mind can also be called the gatekeeper of our minds. You can think of it as a filter, which allows both good and evil things to get through. It is your right to choose what you want. This will be discussed further.

If someone tries to convince you of a belief, your conscious will filter that belief. If someone told you that the sky was orange, your subconscious mind would immediately filter or reference your lifetime experience and knowledge to determine that it is not true. This statement, "The skies are orange", wouldn't make it to the gate.

Subconscious Mind

Your subconscious mind is the part responsible for all involuntary activities. Your subconscious mind controls all bodily functions, including breathing, digestion, heartbeat, and digestion.

Your conscious mind will control your rate of breathing if it is increased or decreased. If you are just breathing naturally without trying to control it, your subconscious mind will control.

Your subconscious mind can also control your emotions. You might feel fearful, anxious, or down sometimes.

Your past lives, beliefs, memories, skills and situations, as well all images you have seen, are vividly stored by your subconscious mind. It holds everything that isn't in your conscious brain.

An example of a person learning the basics of driving a car is a good way to understand her subconscious mind. She would not be able communicate with anyone at the beginning while driving. In an emergency, she would instead be concentrating her attention on learning and mastering how to operate a vehicle. It would be dangerous for her to have a conversation at this point. This is because she still uses her conscious brain to drive from the start. However, driving becomes more instinctive and she no longer has to think about it. This happens because her subconscious mind learns to drive and frees up memory.

How to combine the subconscious mind and the conscious

It is easy to grasp the differences between the conscious or unconscious mind by doing a simple exercise. Begin by slowing down your breathing and holding it. Now, you can relax your body by exhaling slowly. While your conscious mind was controlling your breath, your conscious body was in control.

You can now let your breath naturally flow by letting go of control. You'll be amazed at the way your subconscious mind returns your normal breathing rate to when you forget about this exercise.

It is useful to understand how the unconscious and conscious minds work together so that you can take advantage of their combined power.

You can train and control your mind naturally when you combine the effectiveness of your sub conscious mind with the seamless power visualization. Here are some tips to help you prepare for Visualization.

Chapter 16: Shape Shift And Transform Your Lives

Daily affirmations

1. I am constantly changing my life, each night and every single day.

2. Each movement and action I take is making me more aware of what I can do and how I can use them.

3. Every day, I take in radiant, positive, transformative energy. And every day, my body lets go.

Tap into the infinite supply of creativity and merge with the ever-changing, refreshing water flow. Hear the messages of the wind and view entire worlds from the flickering light of a candle. You can make it all possible by learning how to shapeshift.

Sometimes regarded as magical and mysterious shape shifting can actually be a natural human ability. It is a language you can communicate with your spirit. This is your innate ability, to shapeshift, transform, or become anything you wish. It is possible to proactively change your life and reach your full potential by awakening and expanding your awareness.

The journey of the shape shifter is an adventure that involves body, spirit and mind. It's a journey of personal discovery, self-empowerment, healing, and positive transformation. As the shape-shifting process allows you to change certain aspects of your lifestyle, personal transformation becomes much easier.

When you start your adventure, be open to new possibilities. Your life's transformation is an exciting experience full of wonder, fascination, joy, and amazement.

Meditations, visualizations, affirmations, meditations, and exercises

Your mind is like your muscle. You can exercise it by using affirmations, meditation, visualization, or mediation. This book allows you to use your eyes closed or open for meditations, visualizations, as well as exercises. For many people, it is easier and more enjoyable to have your eyes closed when they are able to experience the experience. It all depends upon what works best for your situation.

Meditating can be done by simply closing your eyes. You can read a few lines each time you open your eyes. Then, close your eyes again to imagine the scenes, actions and suggestions. A partner can be your family member, friend or relative. Another option is recording the visualizations, meditations, or exercises on an electronic device you prefer, and playing them back.

Daily affirmations can be used to remind you to do your best every day. These affirmations can be written on index cards, slips of writing, or on slips. You can then keep them in a bulletin board, refrigerator, at your television or on your computer. To get the best results, you should read the affirmation(s), at least 9 times per hour for 21 days.

These meditations, visualizations and exercises are not recommended for use while driving or operating any machinery or appliances. Your electronic devices may be used in shape shifting meditations, visualizations and exercises. This could include your smartphone, tablet or tape recorder.

You might also find it useful to keep a notepad or record of your experiences and impressions with shape shifting. Make a few short notes after each one. These notes will clarify your thoughts and help you to move faster.

Meditation on Mindfulness

This easy meditation will help shift your awareness. Mindfulness can improve your mind, body and spirit. It lowers stress levels, blood pressures, anxiety, worry, as well as the risk of developing heart attacks. It increases awareness, consciousness, self-esteem, and self-confidence. Deepak Chopra explains in his book Super Brain: "When you close the eyes and turn inward, even for just a few minutes," your brain will reset. This is how your personal transformation begins.

Start by sitting straight. Move your feet forward and cross your hands. To center your awareness, close the eyes and take a deep, full breath in and out. Now, take another deep and complete breathe and think about where you really enjoy being in nature.

Take another deep breath. Now, imagine yourself being in your favorite part of nature.

Think about how you feel when you are in your favorite place in nature. Take another deep breath. Allow yourself to be enchanted by the natural beauty, splendor and energy of this special place.

You can take another deep, complete, and exhale. This will bring the feeling of relaxation, enjoyment, and joy to the present moment.

Take another deep breath. Next, open your eyes. Bring that sense of relaxation and peace to the present moment.

After you are done, you can write down your thoughts on the meditation in your notebook.

Reinventing Yourself

The beauty of shape-shifting is that you don't have to be a professional. All you need are the will and ability and the will to merge and become one with the cosmic flow. By changing your intention, your perception of reality is altered. Your awareness experiences dramatic and permanent changes.

Energy shape shifting is the type you'll be doing. The nonphysical energy body is a complex and coherent energy system. It responds directly to your thoughts. The form and shape you take on is created by your thoughts. You can change your life by shaping your thoughts, emotions and actions.

As with all things, the more that you practice shapeshifting, the better you will be at it. I have included numerous new age meditations. Visualizations and affirmations. Also, body, mind and spirit exercises. You can also use these self-help methods to shapeshift.

You can shape shift and experience constant change in your world. Think about how you already spend some of your daily time in alternate worlds when you're sleeping or dreaming. It is something you do without even trying.

By the simple act of being alive, you experience constant body, mind,and spirit shape shifting. Every second there are physical changes that occur on a cellular basis in your body. Aging is the most prominent of these. Cells multiply and divide constantly and your physical form changes over time. These physical changes also invariably bring about mental or spiritual changes.

When your mental outlook or perception changes, you change shape and become a changed person. Shape shifting is possible in spiritual applications through meditation, visions (divine communication), dream, ritual, prayer and meditation. Many of these experiences can transform the fabric of your life.

Oneness and cosmic consciousness

The ability to shapeshift allows you to transcend the structures and forces that keep your Earthly plane grounded. By doing this, you can move to a space where time and place become fluid and flexible, creating a gateway into oneness, where all things join together in one consciousness.

Carl Jung described this oneness in the "cosmic consciousness". Once you have reached this level, your perspective will change and shift. Once you have crossed that threshold, everything becomes more malleable. This makes it possible to make things change. You will experience a transformation that extends into every area of your life.

Energy patterns make up everything and everything. This causes and affects a variety of changes in our beings that transform and change who and what we become over time. All things are connected by a huge web, which is interwoven with the oneness pattern. Everybody on this planet has been or will be a part of the web. This web influences all aspects and characteristics. It also imprints energy and contributes to its existence.

String Theory lends credence to the notion that there is a cosmic interwoven web which connects into one. String Theory posits that all vibrations are generated by tiny loops or energetic strings. These strings create a web that looks like a spider's web with their filamentary, needle-like structures.

Astronomers have captured the image now of a web-like structure made of filaments that connect all galaxies within the universe. They call this web-like structure the cosmic web.

Shape shifting is a way to tap into this energy web. Expanding your awareness and becoming more open and receptive for different energy types opens up dimensions that you may not have thought of before.

The Shape Shifting Grail Quest

You can shape shift into a jaguar to move through the jungle. It also has the ability to see everything through its eyes, similar to the mythological Grail search. Both shapeshifting and the Grail quest require you to embark on an adventure to find personal insights and divine wisdom. It is an adventure that will lead to transformation and promote personal growth. Like all quests, shape shifting opens doors to new realms and allows you to discover more about yourself.

These are the basic elements of shape shifting.

A person who needs to change

Unconscious state in which the mind is altered and the body takes on a new shape.

The personal and/or psychological transformation that comes from the experience of shaping your body

These are the essential components of shape shifting. Begin with someone in need for change in their life. Next, trigger something that causes the person to shift form. Additionally, you need to be open and willing to change.

Movies featuring popular shape shifters

Hollywood has always loved the idea of shape-shifting. Many times, Hollywood draws from mythology folklore and fairytales. Many films revolve around a main character seeking help. After undergoing a shapeshifting experience, the transformation transforms his/her life.

Many shape-shifting characters are featured in Disney's magic kingdom of cartoons, television series, and movies. Many of these films touch upon the three elements involved with shape shifting. Cinderella is a great example. Cinderella suffers abuse from her stepmother and stepsisters. She is desperate for help. Cinderella is able to transform her life and become a strong and attractive woman thanks to her Fairy Godmother. Her success attracts the admiration of the prince. The shoe fit her, she leaves her evil stepmother behind, takes it off, and she becomes a princess. It was a most positive, successful shape-shift!

Beauty and the Beast is another example. The magical abilities of an old woman transform the handsome prince, who is devoid of love and compassion, into a horrifying Beast. He is told by her to find someone to love him or risk being a Beast forever.

The story's heroine, the youngest daughter a merchant has lost his fortune, is the protagonist. A merchant travels to the garden where the Beast grows roses. If he does not send one of his daughters, he is likely to die. Beauty, the youngest, offers to go to Beast and discovers that the beast she lives with is a generous and noble creature.

Beauty goes to her father to see him, but when Beauty expresses her love for him, the spell is broken. Beauty is then freed from the Beast-form and becomes the prince. More importantly, he discovers the nature and essence of love, an emotion buried deep within himself. Again, these three elements emerge: the desire for change, a transformational experience that changes the shape of the body, and the empowerment that results.

The Shaggy Dog's original Disney film portrays Wilby Daniels as a shy, awkward teenager in search of help. Wilby is a troubled teenager who finds the Borgia family magic ring. He puts it on the finger of his finger, says the magic spell, and transforms into an enormous shaggy dog. His perception of life changes and he saves the young girl from the evil guys. This makes him more confident and self-assured. This story demonstrates the three main elements of form shifting.

Another famous example is the movie It's a Wonderful Life. George Bailey, the main character in the film, has to deal with a crisis. Clarence appears at the exact moment George is about to commit suicidal suicide. Clarence manipulates George to transform him into another reality. George can view his "old reality" and see the world from a different perspective in this alternate reality. George's perspective changes when he experiences this. George, when Clarence restores him to his normal existence uses his shape shifting experience for transcending his personal crisis.

Jake Sully (the main character in Avatar) is a recent Hollywood example. Jake Sully is a paraplegic that longs to have a fully functional body. Jake takes on the Avatar body, and is transformed into a new being with new strengths and powers. As he is one with the divine life force in this new world, he discovers a whole new world. After helping the native people to save their planet from an evil, brutal corporation, he decides that the Avatar transformation is permanent.

Chapter 17: Procrastination & Stagnation: Why Our Lives Are Stagnated

"All life must be in constant, continuous motion." It is death if there is no such motion.

-"Unknown Author"

If you allow a pillar of your life to stay constant beyond the "healthy-for-you-margin", the universe will have no choice than to throw your life out of equilibrium.

A life that is not moving is called a stagnant life. The everyday energy you need for life to continue moving forward becomes zero energy. It is similar to disengaging all of the gears in a car in order to push it downhill. Your life is not flowing with positive or harmful energy if it becomes stagnant. When your life lacks a clear source of energy, it becomes more susceptible to influences from the energy around you.

Your energy can be affected by negativity. Therefore, negativity is more likely to surround you.

There are many reasons our lives can stagnate. Two main causes of stagnation are: These are:

The lack of motivation to improve, Satisfaction with the status quo.

Anticipation for better i.e. You can wait and hope for the best, but do nothing to make your life better.

It is important to remember that even though waiting and hoping for something better sounds like an effective plan, it is usually referred to simply as letting fate (or destiny) take its course. This is analogous to being in prison. If you allow 'waiting to see' to be a part your every day life, you will not be surprised at the opportunities that come along.

Stagnation is like being in prison. The guards must tell the prisoner what to do and where to go. You are letting go of control over your life when it becomes stagnant or unproductive due to the factors mentioned above, and other factors that can lead to stagnation.

Everybody has their best intentions. Your life is stagnant. Essentially, you have given up control and become complacent with what is happening. So who are you letting go of control and how can they steer your life in the right direction?

There are two main causes for life stagnation, as we mentioned above. A lack of motivation is at the top of this list. Motivation is referred to as 'willpower'. Willpower (subconscious brain) and willpower (conscious body) are necessary to change, become or achieve something. If you lose motivation, your life will become empty of any plan or objective. Your reason for being here is lost. Some people may see a life without a plan, or objective as a dream.

If we are honest, most stagnation and procrastination in our lives is due to a lack or motivation. Stagnation and procrastination can be explained by consensually choosing not to allow certain emotions, aspects, and projects to change and fill in the void.

Let's face it, while most of us understand and are well aware of the dangers of stagnation or contentment with the status-quo, most of our brains are constantly working to maintain our mental health by creating 'busywork' that occupy our mental faculties. These busy-tasks are excuses that only cement our stagnation.

Stagnation is "just-waiting-around." You should note that waiting is a normal occurrence in life. Just because it's normal does not necessarily mean it is healthy. Negative emotions such as fear, which are often the cause of waiting, are most common. If you're familiar with the law o f attraction or like attracts kind, you will be able to see that negative energy breeds positive energy.

In itself, stagnation is a lack of motivation. It's not easy to cultivate the ability to be motivated. The fact that life is fluid means that you can never be certain of what the next shoe will drop. Consistent daily effort is necessary to overcome stagnation. Motivation can give you the energy and motion to adapt to the changes in life.

As it happens, procrastination or stagnation in life can be a result of personal choices. You can either be stagnant in your life or procrastinate because it is what you allow.

A stagnant brain is one that has a disconnect or conflict between the 'will' and 'power' of your subconscious and conscious minds. If these two parts of a person's being are in conflict, there is no way to bring about positive change.

The choice between procrastination, stagnation, and both is yours. You can choose to accept the status quo, or wait for fate to happen, in a situation like this. You decide to accept the situation as it is, consciously or subconsciously.

Stigma and procrastination have become epidemics. Personal development research has shown that two out of ten people have at least dealt with one of these aspects of life. While the numbers are not tangible, there is personal growth research.

There is light at both the end of the tunnel and the good news isn't always as bad as you think. In fact, there are thousands of people all over the world who stop allowing fate or fate to control their lives. Instead, they take control of their lives through one thing: staying motivated.

How can I stay motivated? There are many ways you can stay motivated, as you work to take back control over your life. Personal development is top on the list. How do you get control of your life with personal development? This is an excellent question. Let's consider it from a more in-depth perspective.

Chapter 18: Mind & Health

After I have helped you understand the most basic and fundamental things about your eating habits, your subconscious mind, and what it is, I will help with the association of your mind and your health.

The subconscious mind is important in maintaining good health. Let me highlight three features of the subconscious that are most relevant to our purpose.

It accepts all facts and ideas that are presented to it

It can think and reason but in a completely different way than the conscious brain

It retains all details of an individual's past events since childhood.

These features can help one uncover the root causes of an individual's emotions or upset mood.

The conscious mind is sometimes called the everyday head'. This is because it is the part of a person's life that is awake at all hours. The conscious mind is responsible for making decisions and transactions. The subconscious mind is open to any suggestions it receives and will act on them. Therefore, whatever you think about yourself and what you do every single day gets stored in your subconscious mind and it follows it.

We know now that reprogramming our subconscious mind is necessary if our goal is to be achieved. When we are asleep and in a relaxed state of mind, our subconscious mind will take control of our body. It might seem strange that you are asking, "How do I do this while I sleep?". This is the reason you are reading this book. This is how I'll teach you relaxation techniques to re-programme the mind. This is the method you can use the rest of your lives. It's similar to learning to swim or cycle. Once you master it, you won't forget it.

Our goal is to get your subconscious mind to change how you eat and to make food more of a friend. You will be able to enjoy food and not just stuff your face with it throughout the day.

Some might wonder what the subconscious mind has to do with eating. In fact, when we fall asleep, our mind remains relaxed and extended. The tensions and toxicities of the person's conscious mind are then released. The subconscious mind then reprograms our actions, and when we wake up, we do the same thing as what we have been programmed to do.

Another thing to keep in mind is setting goals for yourself and reprogramming your mind to reach them. Realistic and achievable goals are essential. It's impossible to reprogram your brain to lose 10 pounds in one night. This is impossible. Our goals must be realistic and achievable. However, transformations do occur but they are not always easy. You need to take small steps towards your goal, not one large leap. It is the same for reprogramming your mind.

Our subconscious mind will be our motivational house, so we need to ensure that it is filled with the right thoughts.

Although we all know how our subconscious mind works to help us achieve our goals, what about our conscious mind. It doesn't take will power or willpower to reprogram our subconscious mind. However, it is necessary to program our conscious mind. Here are some helpful and thoughtfully chosen tips to help you reach your goals.

Good eating habits

Tip #1 – Eat less but eat at regular times. You can't expect anyone to take your food away so don't treat food like a burden.

Tip 2 - Take small bites while you eat small portions. You should enjoy each bite of food. This will make the meal more enjoyable.

Tip #3 – Make it a routine to keep portions on your plates after you are satisfied. Don't overeat, as this can lead to upset stomachs the next morning.

Tip 4 - Don't watch TV, use your phone or laptop while eating. If you are distracted while eating, you don't absorb the flavors of the food and your taste buds do not respond to them. Finding satisfaction in food is a sign that you will eat more. You're wrong. Once you make the right corrections, you will be able again to enjoy your food.

Tip #5- Who doesn't feel hungry? For those cravings to be satisfied, eat a healthy and delicious snack.

Tip #6 -- If your cravings are not satisfied, have the food you desire but in a smaller amount. Refrain from all distractions as described in tip #4. Instead, use tip 2.

Tip #7- While it would be unfair to ask you if you have cut down on high-calorie foods, I suggest to reduce the amount of calories. Take small amounts of the food you like.

Tip #8- Get more active. If you don't like exercising, try moving around more. It is also a good idea to choose walking over taking public transport if you're going to a nearby place. This will allow you to burn calories and save money on fuel.

It isn't a crash diet, but you might be wondering. These are simply new eating habits to replace the ones you have been using. I have not listed what you should and shouldn't eat. Instead, I have shown how to properly eat your food.

You have now learned how your subconscious and conscious minds can work together to reach your goals. Next, you will learn how relaxation works and how to reprogram your subconscious with your desired image, eating habits, or thoughts.

Let's start with another list of activities. Make sure to always have a pen and a notebook with you.

Assignment 3 - I need you to imagine your ideal body image. Be practical with your choice and then write about it in your notebook.

Assignment 4 - I need you to weigh your body right now. Write down today's date along with your weight. You can also write the weight you wish to achieve by the end you have used all of these techniques.

This will be your daily time. You'll now set a specific time and weigh in once per week. This will become your progress scale.

Assignment 5: List the most visited places in your area. Make it a point that you walk to these locations instead of using other modes.

Assignment 6 - Stock up on healthy and yummy snacks for your sweet tooth.

Assignment 7: List out the high-calorie foods and drinks you frequently consume. The next time that you have them, make a conscious decision not to eat as many of them. Gradually, your consumption of high-calorie food will decrease.

What's the point of eating this?

You should ask one simple question whenever you start to eat.

"Why am i eating this?"

Surprisingly, most of the time, you won't be able give an answer to this question. If you find yourself feeling hungry between meals, and you are constantly looking for food, think about this question. Instead of eating food that is not necessary, take three deep breaths, close your eyes, and visualize your ideal body.

When you are eating at a party, playing cards, or watching television, the same question should be asked. Now, take a deep inhale and ask the question "WHY AM I Eating THIS?"

Be aware of the times you experience these little hunger pangs. You might see a pattern. This can help to modify your meal time and create a better one. You should ask yourself another question if the hunger persists between meals.

"Why is it that I feel like eating at this moment?"

It is up to you to find the root cause and devise a healthy solution.

This will allow you to be more responsible and help you realize why you were eating things you didn't need.

People may try to ridicule or push negative views and opinions on you. However, you must not let anyone get in the way of your goal. Don't be defeated by the opinions of others.

Right now, your only goal is to lose weight, get fit and feel better.

The chapters ahead are important because they hold the key method to master yourself and reprogrammed your subconscious. Continue reading the book with all your attention and focus. Keep in mind that these are little steps to help you achieve your wellness and life goals.

Chapter 19: The Elements Of The Unique Sub-Conscious Mind

Rush has a scene in which James Hunt (played here by Chris Hemsworth), imagines how he will drive along a particular track. He was able to see with his mind the sharp curves as well as the wide bends. And what he would do when he got around those bends. With his eyes closed he pulled the imaginary gear and pressed on the accelerator. He was able to do everything he wanted and he won the actual race. The most fascinating thing about his performance was the fact that he was subconsciously driving. He relied heavily on what he imagined rather than driving consciously.

A swimmer once spent a few moments before every competition to lie down and sleep. But he wasn't sleeping. He was imagining what the swimming competition would look like and how it will end. This, of course is a victory he will claim.

Both cases share one common factor: visualization. This is one method to tap into your subconscious mind to program it for what you want. When visualization is done regularly, it can change your perspective and alter the course in your life. Ever wonder why you have trouble becoming rich even though all you want is money and more money. It is possible that there is a part in your sub-conscious blocking you from achieving your goals. It is possible to tap and change the reality that exists in your sub-conscious mind.

What exactly is the subconscious mind?

The mind can be represented by an iceberg. Its visible portion is the conscious mind. The sub-conscious part, the big chunk at its bottom, is what would be called the unconscious mind. The sub-conscious could be the key to your success. It did sink Titanic. After all, it is the ship representing the obstacles that prevent you from reaching your goals.

According to psychological perspectives, the subconscious is that part that is not in focal consciousness. It is wrong to say that it is unaware. Only that it needs to become more focused is the truth. It functions as a memory vault that keeps all of your memories safe. It can store and retrieve data and help you to achieve your dreams and goals.

The sub-conscious is responsible for many things, including quick recall and access.

Memories

Are you supposed to remember the phone number of someone? Did you ever wonder how you could drive a car with no conscious thought? All details are stored in the memories of your brain, which the sub-conscious can tap into whenever you need.

Daily Programs You Can Run

These include your thoughts, values, beliefs, habits, and behaviors. Sub-consciousness processes information and then validates it with regard to your actual perception.

Sensations & their meanings

The subconscious, which taps into the unconscious side of your mind, attempts to make sense out of your 5 senses. The unconscious is directly connected to the subconscious.

You might be surprised at how it can transform your life.

Your brain's "autopilot" is the subconscious mind. You will automate your behavior and thinking patterns as they become more established. It means that if you create good habits that lead you to success, you won't have to think hard or put in much effort. However, to truly harness the power of the sub-conscious mind and its many secrets, it is necessary to be aware of them. It can't process negatives. It doesn't know the word not so telling yourself that you won't gain weight again and again will have the reverse effect. Your sub-conscious will record it as "I will gain more weight". A better solution is to tell your self that you are healthy, happy, or beautiful and slim. These thoughts will become part of your subconscious and you will engage in activities that will help turn them into reality.

Making money is no different. If you keep thinking "I'm poor", you will become miserable all the time. You won't see any other ways to improve your situation. They said it was all in the mind. This statement is even more true for the sub-conscious. The following will help you get an idea of how your subconscious can take you from zero to her.

You can see the sub-conscious thoughts that are preventing you from becoming a better person.

Know your goals and then refocus.

Always be grateful

A Quick Factor on Subconsciousness

To tap your subconscious mind and program it, the first step is to become familiar with its processes.

It cannot tell the difference between real and imagined, which is why it continues to serve the conscious, despite having amazing powers.

If the subconscious mind has believed in something for longer periods of time, it will be much more difficult to alter that belief.

It acts on the premise of every thought having a physical response. If you think you are performing badly, you will feel your heart race and have trouble breathing.

This can lead to unrealistic expectations. This may sound crazy but it's true. If you expect to fail, you're likely to fail. Your subconscious will work hard for you to succeed.

It is often able to prevail over the conscious in terms if there are conflicts. Fear will set in when you enter a darkened room, even if you attempt to convince yourself that the area is safe.

It holds an accepted idea forever, until it can be replaced by something new.

It cannot be programmed by suggestions or hypnosis.

You will find it much easier to tap into your sub-conscious mind, and harness its power in order to make a difference in your life.

Chapter 20: Illustration Of Creative Visualization By Wallace Wattles

Wallace Wattles, a bestselling author of The Science of Getting Rich (1910), described visualization. Every person who has ever been interested in the power to mind is aware of him or has read this work. The Science of Getting Rich (1910) was a phenomenal success story and is still the most read book. This book continues to enjoy the same level of popularity it enjoyed 100 years ago.

The Science of Getting Rich (1910) - The author shares his thoughts and insights on how to be rich and get anything you want. Wattles invented creative visualization. This thought process literally paved the way for a movement. Napoleon Hill was one of his many inspirations. The ideas he shared about creative visualization are the foundation of "The Secret", as well as the book.

Wallace Wattles said that all of life comes from our thoughts. The thought process governs the universe. Whatever we think in life becomes larger and more materialistic.

Wallace claims that if we believe that we will live in a new home, wear fine clothes, drive a vehicle for our daily travels, we will be able to feel confident about all things. He advises us to visualize the perfect environment and financial stability and then live it every day. He says this will lead to the positive change in your life.

Wattles observed that an individual's ability to reciprocate thoughts or beliefs can have an effect on the creation or development of the substance.

He believes that it is essential to remain focused on one's goal or set of goals until the end. He or she should keep the goal in mind and accept it as hard reality. Once you have determined your goal, it is time to start thinking about how you can achieve it. The universe will take it as its reality if you think it again and again.

You must be clear about the goal you are pursuing and continue to think about it. Avoid dwelling on your present circumstances and situations, which could hinder your efforts towards success.

Wallace Wattles said that it is important to be grateful for all the things you have. Gratitude connects us with the power. People can give it the names of God, Spirit or Divine. This energy or connection facilitates visualization manifestations or changes. Gratitude opens up your vibration points, and you can be open to acceptance or openmindedness.

Wallace Wattles claims that success can be achieved by combining many different things. It is important to be grateful for all those things that contributed to your success.

Chapter 21: Mobile Web And The Internet: The Advancement Of The Internet

Mobile devices, as well as computers, have become an integral part in our daily lives. We are connected digitally to the internet, which gives us instant access virtually anywhere in the world.

These creative thinkers are responsible for this. Yet, the Internet has created a platform that will allow a whole generation of creatives to succeed. We can learn a lot from them for those with more technical skills.

Michael Heyward, founder & CEO of Whisper

Right now, privacy and anonymity seem to be sacred concepts. Whisper has been introduced to an online world in which everyone wants your data. Whisper, a mobile app that lets users confess their secrets with anonymity, is called Whisper. As if you were in a confessional with millions and millions of priests, but don't know what you are.

Whisper was invented by Michael Heyward to stop digital trails getting to their end. Users simply type in a secret, and it is then overlayed on a relevant photo. The content is then uploaded to a shared database, which is accessible to millions more users every day. Whisper doesn't allow users to create profiles or follow other users. Communication is done through private messages and anonymous replies. It's possible to remain completely anonymous if this is what you desire.

What app boasts 3.5 Billion page views per month that surpasses the New York Times website every quarter? That's right, Whisper.

Michael Heyward demonstrates that it is possible to fight unwanted intrusions from any level with just a simple rebuttal...even with whispers.

CoFounders Tinder: Justin Mateen and Sean Rad

Sometimes innovation doesn't have to be about creating new concepts, but rather about simplifying existing ideas.

Justin and Sean were looking for a simpler way to go about online dating. In order to find potential love interests, traditional online dating sites require you to create a profile and answer lots of questions. This method isn't suitable for all people. Sometimes the profiles are so lengthy that they don't allow for much discussion during the "get know you" phase. People who aren't open to detailed communication may be left in the dark about a lot.

Tinder is a smartphone app that reduced the dating site profile to one photo and simplified initial communication to a simple swipe. Justin states that this interface "captures when your eyes connect to someone."

Tinder's app guarantees mutual attraction as it only notifies both parties if they swipe right. This simplicity has proved to be a success with Tinder attracting 10 million users each day and 750 million swipes. Justin and Sean intend to improve the app by adding fun and lighter-hearted features in near future.

Tim Kendall is Head of Product for Pinterest

Pinterest is huge. But you don't necessarily need to be an Internet and Social Media expert. This is because Pinterest can be very smart if your company is targeted at women. Why? It's because 80% of Pinterest users, 92% of whom are women, use Pinterest to pin items. Pinterest has proven its ability to influence markets online and offline. Cha-ching!

How does Tim Kendall play a role in this? Tim Kendall was the Head Of Product at Pinterest. He was instrumental in launching the Pinterest App for iPhone, Android and Tablets in 2013. It wasn't only the release of apps, it was also the fact that mobile apps allow pins to display more information for users. This resulted in a huge increase in Pinterest traffic. 75% now come from mobile devices.

Tim took something that worked and improved it. He then made it portable which added tremendous value to an already enormous company.

Alan Schaaf Founder of Imgur

Content is the key to the Internet. The term content was used in the past to mean written content. Once images became popular on multiple levels, such as entertainment, marketing and engagement, their power was evident. It's more than being able to upload images online. Also, sharing images is very popular.

Social Media has taken over the internet but old mediums such as message boards, forums, or social bookmarking sites, like Reddit.com, are still very popular. Most platforms don't permit image uploads. Imgur is an image host.

Alan has gone to great efforts to ensure Imgur is the most popular image hosting site. It offers many features such as commenting and private messages between users. It's also available for users who don't want to log in, and can simply click the Next button to view images.

Imgur receives 130 million unique hits each month. It is also a treasure trove of viral images, memes, and more. It's basically a social networking site for image sharing. Imgur has become a popular site thanks to Alan's innovations.

Alan shows us that it is possible to use the same ideas as another person and make it more valuable by changing it. He has been paying attention to Imgur's growth and has modified it to better suit its audience.

Chapter 22: Why Should You Get Used To Changes

How do you adjust to change?

We are habit-driven. We are used a routine. It is how we get up in the morning, what foods we eat, and what hairstyles we wear. How do you live in that country? What customs do you follow to make money? What we call habits is what we are used too. Every day is full of habits, both good and poor. It is rare that someone will make a change if they don't have a convincing reason or a motivating incentive.

We have a problem dealing with change. No matter how big or small the change is, there will always be discomfort. The extent of the change, and the resistance against it, will determine the severity and duration of the discomfort. Many people are reluctant to change due to the discomfort.

It is uncomfortable to do something you don't normally do. You will soon feel the discomfort and return to doing it as you are accustomed. Anything that isn't what we do every day is difficult. Place a homeless person in the home of a multimillionaire where he enjoys the lifestyle of the wealthy and famous. While he might initially enjoy some of the amenities, he will soon be able to sneak out and return to the street. He is used a different lifestyle and has different habits as a millionaire. He feels uncomfortable living in a totally different way to what he is used.

To make any changes in your life or around you, you must be willing to do so. Your subconscious mind is part of this. Your body reacts to any change you make in your life or yourself. If you're not returning to your routine, the discomfort can increase. You'll feel the discomfort for as long as you don't adjust to the change.

Let's assume that you have set a goal and worked hard to achieve it. However, everything seems against your efforts and you can't get there. You may not realize that there is something you fear about or something you like about the goal. This could be because you are afraid about the discomfort that changes bring. We fear what we don't understand and this is why our system is so strong at avoiding change. You have to quickly return to your previous status if you are experiencing discomfort. You will know why you didn't succeed in making a change in your own life. Your system wants to keep your comfortable zone.

Older people are not interested in having anything replaced with new. They prefer to keep things the way they are. You might wonder why they would accept hardship before changing. This is because it's easier for people to get used and comfortable with the worst, while not having to deal with something completely new.

Perhaps you think you know what you want. Perhaps you are familiar with the car you want and have driven it. Although you may be familiar with the car, do you feel it when you drive it? The higher costs associated with owning the car or the possibility of it being stolen might make you think unconsciously. It could be a car you can't park off the street. Instead, you have to park in an enclosed garage or take over a protected parking space. It's possible that you will be jealous of strangers and friends.

It is much easier to adapt to living with less money than it is to have a lot. It is easier to adjust to having more money than you were used too. It's important to decide what you will do and where to invest the money. Spending money on charity is necessary. There is the fear of losing your money and being robbed.

However, there's more to it. Fears of being able to make more money could cause you to be afraid that people will come begging to you, that your work might be longer and that you might end up becoming more well-known. You might have to change how you dress or behave. People will be friendlier to you, and you won't know the difference between friendly and rude people if you are rich. Your system may say you don't see any problem with this.

Be aware that not all information about a specific money goal can be trusted. All of this is what your system wants to avoid. Visualizing is part, of course. To make the change easier, there are other things you can do.

A person who wants to lose weight must change his eating habits. He should eat different foods and eat smaller portions than before. When you eat smaller portions, it can lead to physical pain as your body adjusts to the lower calorie intake and reduced food choices. It's too hard on the body when a person alters the foods they eat and reduces his calorie intake. The body is able to withstand strong resistance and feel pain.

This is why people often abandon a diet they like and return to the old ways of eating.

One or a few foods can be changed at a time to help someone lose weight. If he waits until he is comfortable eating new foods, then he will change to other foods. Only then, he will get used and won't go back to his old eating patterns. Similar steps should be taken for reducing calories and the amount of food. If he used to eat 2500 calories a day, he can reduce it to 2300 calories. Then he can wait until his body is used to 2300 calories. Then he could reduce the calories intake to 2100 and 2000 calories. After his body adjusts to the decreased food intake, the change would be easy.

Part B of the course will teach you how you can become the person you desire to be once you have reached your big goal. You will become your ideal self, and you will learn to accept it. This will allow you to achieve your big goal. You'll take small steps and not try to do everything at once. It's almost impossible for it to be completely different overnight. It is easier and more effective to make small changes one at a while. You can feel the discomfort diminish quickly by making small changes.

These examples show how you can break down a large goal into smaller components. You can make it easier to follow each step in the process of achieving a huge goal. You can change your eating habits by taking it step-by-step. You can start small, making one change at a given time. Then, take it slow and get used to it. You can also make more money and live in a larger house or do whatever you want.

Take a look at your most important wishes. What is the most important thing you wish you could have?

Let's assume that you want success in business and you desire to make more as an artist. However you are afraid to give up something that you are used to. You are not comfortable with the idea of running your own business, and all its responsibilities. You don't enjoy being a part of events and having to be present at the success stories. It's a scary thought to be forced to work harder. You worry about making investment decisions. You are uncomfortable with the idea that you must choose a higher lifestyle. This includes hiring employees and traveling first class.

Imagine all the possibilities that come with your goals, wishes and desires. You'll feel the changes. You'll find that you like the things you fear, the things you dislike, the things you don't know, and the things you aren't used to.

Every change brings with it some discomfort that your body wants to avoid.

The Solution

1. Do small changes until you feel comfortable with the situation.

2. Accept the discomfort and change that comes with it

HOW TO CHANGE

How can you make it through a major change?

Answer: Just accept little changes.

Try to do one or more things every day differently than you're used to. You'll soon become comfortable with small changes. It will be easier to accept larger changes.

Keep making small changes and, from time to another, make a bigger impact.

Make it a habit of doing something new every day. It is enjoyable and will make it much easier to make more changes.

Attention: By making a little change, I don't mean to make it permanent. This means that you do something different from your usual routine once a week or every other day and then go back to your old ways. It is going to be hard at first. If you do something new than you used, you may feel discomfort. As you become more comfortable with changes, the discomfort will lessen. Changes will become much easier.

When you get used to having coffee on your desk every morning, it is easy to forget about it. It's much more simple to sip water instead. Although you have something to grab, the coffee's flavor is gone.

A bartender is not likely to know your preferences and habits. You must tell the bartender what kind of drink you prefer. You don't know anyone at the bar, so you must think about how to start a conversation. It's not clear if the people you are talking to are safe or dangerous.

If you take another street to get from work or the market, you may not know whether there is more traffic or if you need to go around one-way streets. It is important that you find your way to another market.

Making small changes will make it harder to miss the things you love, hate or fear. It is easier to deal with the discomfort of minor changes. Once you get used to it, it will become easier to handle the bigger changes.

Try to think for at most one day about what you might do differently from the way you are used. When you feel uncomfortable, don't lose heart. Be strong! It will get easier to make small adjustments over time.

By making small changes throughout your day, you can stop being a slave for your old habits. While positive habits are great, you'll only continue to repeat the same old things year after year. Try to include some variety in your positive habits.

Keep your mind open to making little changes throughout your day if you want to be flexible, both mentally and physically, well into old age.

How can you get some ideas on small changes you could make?

Just before you start doing something, ask yourself if it is possible to do it differently. It is possible to do this differently one or several times. After that, you can go back and continue your routine.

What does it take to be successful with small changes?

Some examples of tiny changes

+ If you are a morning person who checks your email early in the day, then do so for one to two days after lunch or at night.

+ You can sleep on your side for a few nights with your head on one side of the mattress.

+ Choose another way to get to work for a day or so, then choose another.

+ Try something new for breakfast. Try something new for lunch. Take a chance on a cuisine that is unfamiliar to you.

+ Make new dishes.

+ You can skip breakfast every now and again, but eat more lunch. Take a bite to eat for dinner and have a bigger breakfast the next morning.

+ Do something after work that you usually don't do. A walk or a coffee shop are two options. If you feel like going for a glass of wine after work, then go straight home.

+ Get up half an-hour earlier than usual and do something that you enjoy during this hour.

+ If you don't eat at a regular table, have a picnic laid out on the floor.

+ Make an effort to visit stores that you are unfamiliar with.

+ If you like to eat on the couch, set the table well for your next meal.

+ Change to another radio channel if you listen to one particular station often.

+ Drive to a grocery store where you have never been before.

+ Meet people with whom you have not been in touch for a while.

+ Meet new people as you travel to different places.

+ Find friends on Facebook and Google+ in other countries to learn about their culture.

+ Rearrange the furniture in one area of your home.

+ Learn a foreign languages, even if only a few phrases.

+ If you are accustomed to watching a TV show, switch to another one for a few more days. Some shows will go unnoticed if you stop watching them daily. You may see something new instead.

+ If you regularly buy a particular magazine or newspaper, then buy another.

+ Change the exercises you do, the time at which you exercise, and how long you workout.

+ Visit another hairdresser as you would normally and ask for a different haircut.

Chapter 23: Different Types Creative Thinking

You will be able to understand the different types of ideas.

There are four types. Arne dietrich (2004) distinguished four distinct types of creativity by comparing different mind exercises. You can think of it as a matrix. Creativity is either cognitively based or candidly. It can also be constrained or unconstrained. The four quadrants are now visible.

1: Thomas Edison:

Cognitive creativity, which is deliberate and intentional, refers to creativity that arises from the support of work in an order. Thomas Edison was an example of a deliberate and creative maker. Before he would create an invention, he tried to test it. Thomas Edison created the phonograph and film camera, in addition to the light. Your pre-frontal cortex, or PFC (prefrontal cortex) is the place where cognitive and deliberate creativity begins. The PFC allows you to do two things:

> Carefully consider and > Make associations between information stored in different parts your brain. In order for cognitive creativity to be deliberate and intentional, you should have a group learning around a few specific points. If you are cognitively creative and intentionally using existing information, you will create new and innovative ways to use it.

2: Personal leap forward 'a-ha' minutes

If you have ever been in a personal crisis (relationship breakup, termination, liquidation) and have gained some insight about yourself and the consequences of your choices, you may have experienced emotional creativity. This kind of creativity includes the PFC. It is the deliberate. People who are engaged in deliberate, emotional creativity do not focus on any one skill or region. Instead, they spend their time exploring feelings and emotions. The brain's cingulated section processes complex sentiments. This is a part that can be identified with how others collaborate and your place on this planet. The PFC is also associated to the cingulated cortex. These brain regions can produce this kind creativity.

3 Isaac Newton "Eureka" Minutes:

Ever worked on an idea or issue that you didn't get the hang of? Perhaps you have struggled to find the right people to help you with a job at work. After you have finished your lunch, you are able to glean a lot of information on how to staff the project. This is a good example of both cognitive and spontaneity.

The brain's basal and cognitive ganglia are both spontaneous and innate. This is the location dopamine is stored, and it is an area of the brain that functions outside of your conscious awareness. The aware brain gives up on the issue in the middle of spontaneous, cognitive creativity. This leaves the brain open to the oblivious and allows them to continue working on it. If you feel that an issue is beyond the scope of your conscious awareness, then you need to remove it from conscious mindfulness. If you do an alternate, inconsequential move, the PFC will be able to interconnect information in new ways using your oblivious mental preparation. As an example of spontaneous and cognitive creativity, the Isaac Newton tale about Newton contemplating gravity as he watched a falling fruit fall is a great example. This kind of creativity is dependent on a continuous collection of information. This is the cognitive portion

4: "Epiphanies":

The amygdala inspires spontaneous and emotional creativity. The amygdala houses fundamental feelings. It is possible to create spontaneous ideas and manifestations when the PFC (the conscious brain) and the aware brain are at rest. This is what you will see in the creative minds of extraordinary craftsmen or performers. These spontaneous and emotional creative moments are extremely powerful, as is an epiphany or religious experience. For this kind of creativity, there is no particular information required (it's certainly not cognitive). However, it is common to have some expertise (written, aesthetic, musical) that will help you make something from your spontaneous and emotional creative ideas.

Creativity levels

To master that process, you need to first understand three key levels of creativity: invention, discovery, and creation.

1. Invention: The highest level creativity is that of invention. Alexander Graham Bell invents the phone, for instance. In any event, you should ask the question: "Would it have been possible to invent the phone without Bell?" The answer is yes. Long-term, the phone would have been invented based on the fact that science existed. Although it might have taken longer to happen, it would have happened. It's not as easy to invent something than discover it, but it's something

that's inevitable. It's possible for someone else to invent it if you don't.

2. Discovery: The lowest level in creativity is discovery. It is, generally speaking, the point where you can be aware of or find something- - - discover it. You might call it "discovered workmanship" if you are a skilled worker. It can be a piece of stone with a unique shape, or a piece of wood with an unusual example. A bit of common stone or woodwork can be purchased as a result of discovered craftsmanship. Many inventions begin with a discovery.

3. Creation: The largest amount of creativity is found in creation. Othello on stage is an example of a genuine creation. Shakespeare would have been the only one to have produced Elizabethan shows, and Othello would not be possible without Shakespeare. You can only make certain things, and that is what your company can do! Finding those things is the key to success.

Chapter 24: Increase Productivity By Creating Specific Habits

Learning to focus will allow you to direct all your attention to the priority. This will help you be more productive at night. Focus and productivity go hand-in-hand, so it is important to establish the following habits.

Follow your morning ritual. According to many productive people, the worst way for a person to start their day is to check their email and plan. Instead, spend your morning focusing on yourself. You should eat breakfast, exercise, and meditate. This will help you be more productive.

Prioritize the hardest task. Prioritize the most challenging task of the day, especially before lunchtime. Do this while you are still full of energy. Focus on the task at hand and don't think about other things. If you make it a habit, you'll always have a productive and fulfilling day.

Manage your distractions. Identify and describe your distractions. Next, find a way to overcome them. Next, you should make it a habit that you manage distractions at every opportunity. For example, if your bad habit is to constantly check your social media and emails at the same time every day, then schedule it so that you only do this once a day. To eliminate temptation, turn off instant notifications.

Do not forget to meditate. Meditation is an important part of our decision-making process. Avoid skipping it as much as you can. Regular meditation can really improve your ability focus.

It is important to take frequent breaks. Experts advise taking a quick 15-minute break each hour to help you stay alert and focused throughout the day. To help you refocus on the things that really matter, you can download an app that blocks you from surfing the web.

You should exercise as often as you can. You might be tempted to check your social media whenever you have the opportunity, but it's better to do something active than that. You should spend no less than 5 minutes each 15-minute break to doing short workouts. YouTube is full of 5 minute video workouts. You can also take a quick walk of 10 to 15 minutes, or perform pushups, squats, and jumping jacks. It can help to take a break, relax and focus on the physical side of things.

At all times, work purposefully. Before you start any task, make a list of your goals and intentions. This will help keep you focused and organized. It is important to set a no-distraction rule. Do not engage in any activity that can distract you for even a second. It will only make your time more wasted than it is worth.

Take a Technology Detox. The internet is a useful tool but it can also be dangerous. This is the most effective way to learn to focus. Unplug your phone every now and again to enjoy activities we used to enjoy before the internet. It is possible to set your smartphone on airplane mode for just an hour during your day. You should also refrain from going online for at least one day a week. You will find it easier to relax your mind and concentrate if it's done more than once.

Chapter 25: The Pickles Must Be Held

Another childhood memory was a commercial for a hamburger place that announced its new double burger. This commercial opened with a catchy little song:

> "Hold on to the pickles
>
> "Hold on to the lettuce
>
> "Special orders don't upset us
>
> "All that is required of us is your cooperation."
>
> "Serve it up your way...
>
> "HAVE it yourRRRRRRRRRRRRRRRRRRRRRRRRRRRRRRRRRRRRRRRRRRRRRRRRRRRRRRRRRRRR...
>
> "It goes double now!"

The commercial went on for a while, the point being that they were there in order to feed us whatever we desired, and double our portions.

Again, this makes me smile. When I think about it now, I see it in terms of Law of Attraction. It is as if the Universe is calling me, reminding to send signals of my true desires--special orders and such! The Universe will fill my order and double the amount I could have come up for details.

I bring this up to highlight the fact that it is important to understand what the ideal life looks and how you can use Tapping, the Law of Attraction, and Visualization to make it happen.

To uncover your beliefs, patterns, disempowering meanings, and habits that have been running in the background, we used the earlier exercises. We'll be using EFT and free flowing tapping on these.

If you have noticed the paradox of EFT focusing on "pain" and you worry that it will send out a "misery-door" signal to the Universe, let me assure you.

It's already sending out the "misery doors" signal about which painful items you're going EFT to. But it's not obvious, because you've become so familiar with it. This is like wearing your sunglasses on your top. You don't notice it and then you start searching for them. Your life has been producing the results you want, and you know it.

EFT rounds are also very fast. This means that even though you focus on the "miserydoor" signal for just a few seconds, the EFT rounds result in it being neutralized quickly and the "miserydoor" signal is shutting down. This allows for the energy flow to be restored and improves the signal. This not only sends out an updated signal in the current moment but also ensures that any "behind the scenes signal" that was sabotaging you efforts is dealt, often permanently. Your "bliss-door" thoughts, feelings, and emotions can be released. From there, the old elephant will cease following his regular, same ol', same ol' routine and become open to your suggestions.

That requires you to figure out what you really want.

Help me Help You

The Universe waits for our signal to let it know what we really want, just as Tom Cruise said in Jerry Maguire. And, as in the opening jingle of the chapter, special orders "are no problem."

This causes a problem when we reference all the things we don't want. This can cause confusion and result in even more disappointing messages.

It's true, many of us have done this to signal our desire for life. By referring to all the things we don't want and/or by asking vaguely for more people, places, or things we do wish for--a.k.a. "I want more money." The Universe will grant you whatever you request, so if you ever believed that or stated that and have never found a penny in the ground, then this is the Universe. You wanted more money. And you got it.

You might be thinking "Yeah, that's what I meant," but the Universe doesn't translate. It only has one job: to match. When you say "I want money more", it's probably because you're looking at your current financial situation and thinking "I don't need enough money." You're sending a signal to the Universe of fear, lack, with a glimmer hope, but mostly doubt. It's not the "bliss-door" signal that you wanted. However, it is the conflicting signal that you sent when you referred to your current situation of lack. This signal goes out to the Universe. It is matched with "more" but not really much more, and voilà! You get a penny. You have more money.

It's not always that obvious and immediate, and I'll talk more about the timing aspect in a moment, but for now, are you starting to see my point about the importance of sending a crystal-clear, referencing-only-that-which-you-want, "bliss door" type signal?

Be careful not to be scared that any thought that crosses your mind will immediately result in more of the same.

You see, your thoughts follow the same rules as your beliefs, so it is almost like you have a shared theme. While there may be an occasional "exception blip", thought or feeling that pops up, the main signals your brain is sending are those thoughts and feelings you constantly engage in. You might watch the news one time and then get caught up with the negativity, but it's actually in opposition to your patterns of viewing or thoughts that the world's a loving place. This isn't a strong signal. You should not spend much time viewing programs that cause you to be upset. If you do, you will feel emotionally depleted and emotional impacted. This will strengthen the signal, and thus send out a stronger one.

This is why I recommend you add all the happy emotions that you can imagine to your visualizing.

Things you watch regularly, the activities you engage in consistently, and even the words that you use all have an effect on how you feel and what your beliefs are. This is something you may want to examine to make sure you know exactly what you want.

Without my stuff, who will I be?

The initial stages of releasing limiting beliefs and old trauma and habits can feel both liberating and frightening.

Because we are familiar with the pain and suffering that it causes. We know it's possible to handle it. It may not be our best life but it's manageable. It may seem difficult or even unpleasant, and there may be many other things. However it is often all we know. Without it, who are we? How will we navigate this life?

Without our stuff we can't really know who or what we are.

You might find it a little scary at first when you are trying to eliminate the patterns and blocks that have been part of your life for so long. As a writer who is paralysed by the first blank page, your initial fear of the unknown could lead you to run back to what you have known, even if you don't like it. It's the old saying, "devil you don't know is better than devil you do".

To overcome this temptation, it's important to be very clear about your goal so that you don't fall into your familiar, unsatisfying, comfort zone.

Your comfort zone is the beginning of your life.

~Neale Donald Walsch

Ordering!

It's a fun way for me to begin putting all the pieces together after clearing away any discomforts from tapping. Inspired by the little commercial, I think the Universe is like a group of employees working together for our orders.

This worksheet is based around the idea that you can order something as simple as food. It can be used to clarify your thoughts about people, places, things, and events in your life.

Divide a sheet of paper into four sections. Then label the quadrants as below:

Top Left: I'd like...

Top Right: Hold...

Bottom Left - Easy on the...

Bottom right: Add additional...

Think of ordering food at a restaurant as ordering. You often specify what you would like to order, and then you add on to the base order to make it even more amazing. Perhaps you have a preference. The waiter might offer you a veggie hamburger. (This is the basic order: I'd like _____.

Then, ask the waiter if he would modify the order to make it as you prefer it. (Remember to hold any pickles that you don't like in your experience. These can be written down to help with emotional clearing. It also helps clarify what you are looking for.

Next, you might ask the waiter to take a moment to help you with something that is usually included with your order. (State what you'd prefer, but maybe just a little.

It is a great way to make your experience better.

This worksheet is fun and easy to use as a starting point when you are establishing your vision and for journal work.

This is also a great way of clarifying your desires. Imagine how your dining experience could be if you gave your order for the veggie burger to the waiter. After a while you call the waiter back to inform him that your decision has changed and that you want nachos. He goes back to his kitchen. The waiter then serves you something that looks delicious. Finally, you're happy with the order. However, you notice other customers who arrived late have already finished their meals, and are getting their desserts. You wonder why your order isn't arriving, and you may even think this is a bad place to eat.

This is another example showing what happens when we send weak, conflicting signals up into the Universe. When we see that what we really want is not coming soon enough, we think the process is slow. This worksheet will help clarify your order so you can send up laser-focused signals in the search for matching.

No Man (or Women) is an Island

You might feel isolated when you are doing this type of work. This is something that I hear quite often from my clients. I wanted it to be brought up. When you can let go your long-held beliefs, and other habits, it can feel like you are the only person on an isolated island. I refer to it as feeling like the world is zigging at you.

This can be treated with tapping or visualizations. Tap for the discomfort. Visualize the relationship experiences you desire and tap to it.

Additionally, it's no coincidence the Law of Attraction includes the word action. I encourage you also to get connected with fellow "ziggers." These people are similar-minded individuals who are also on a journey of selfdiscovery. It's easy to connect with people these days. Consider joining my Friends Circle. Maybe you want to start a group within your community of people who have read this guide and will be supporting each other by making changes. A Mastermind group could be as small as one person, or as large and varied as you choose. It's important to surround yourself and others so you can cheer one another on as you go through your transformation.

www.ingramcontent.com/pod-product-compliance
Lightning Source LLC
Chambersburg PA
CBHW050026130526
44590CB00042B/1922